Wiley FRM Exam Review Study Guide 2017
Part I, Volume 1

Wiley FRM Exam Review Study Guide 2017
Part I, Volume 1

Foundations of Risk Management, Quantitative Analysis

Christian H. Cooper, CFA, FRM

WILEY

Cover image: Loewy Design
Cover design: Loewy Design

Copyright © 2017 by John Wiley & Sons, Inc. All rights reserved.

Published by John Wiley & Sons, Inc., Hoboken, New Jersey.
Published simultaneously in Canada.

No part of this publication may be reproduced, stored in a retrieval system, or transmitted in any form or by any means, electronic, mechanical, photocopying, recording, scanning, or otherwise, except as permitted under Section 107 or 108 of the 1976 United States Copyright Act, without either the prior written permission of the Publisher, or authorization through payment of the appropriate per-copy fee to the Copyright Clearance Center, Inc., 222 Rosewood Drive, Danvers, MA 01923, (978) 750-8400, fax (978) 646-8600, or on the Web at www.copyright.com. Requests to the Publisher for permission should be addressed to the Permissions Department, John Wiley & Sons, Inc., 111 River Street, Hoboken, NJ 07030, (201) 748-6011, fax (201) 748-6008, or online at http://www.wiley.com/go/permissions.

Limit of Liability/Disclaimer of Warranty: While the publisher and author have used their best efforts in preparing this book, they make no representations or warranties with respect to the accuracy or completeness of the contents of this book and specifically disclaim any implied warranties of merchantability or fitness for a particular purpose. No warranty may be created or extended by sales representatives or written sales materials. The advice and strategies contained herein may not be suitable for your situation. You should consult with a professional where appropriate. Neither the publisher nor author shall be liable for any loss of profit or any other commercial damages, including but not limited to special, incidental, consequential, or other damages.

For general information on our other products and services or for technical support, please contact our Customer Care Department within the United States at (800) 762-2974, outside the United States at (317) 572-3993 or fax (317) 572-4002.

Wiley publishes in a variety of print and electronic formats and by print-on-demand. Some material included with standard print versions of this book may not be included in e-books or in print-on-demand. If this book refers to media such as a CD or DVD that is not included in the version you purchased, you may download this material at http://booksupport.wiley.com. For more information about Wiley products, visit www.wiley.com.

Library of Congress Cataloging-in-Publication Data:

ISBN 978-1-119-38563-9 (paperback); ISBN 978-1-119-38559-2 (ebk);
ISBN 978-1-119-38560-8 (ebk)

Printed in the United States of America

10 9 8 7 6 5 4 3 2 1

Contents

How to Study for the Exam — ix

About the Instructor — x

Foundations of Risk Management

Lesson: Michel Crouhy, Dan Galai, and Robert Mark, *The Essentials of Risk Management*, 2nd Edition (New York: McGraw-Hill, 2014). Chapter 1. Risk Management: A Helicopter View (Including Appendix 1.1) — 3

Lesson: Michel Crouhy, Dan Galai, and Robert Mark, *The Essentials of Risk Management*, 2nd Edition (New York: McGraw-Hill, 2014). Chapter 2. Corporate Risk Management: A Primer — 9

Lesson: Michel Crouhy, Dan Galai, and Robert Mark, *The Essentials of Risk Management*, 2nd Edition (New York: McGraw-Hill, 2014). Chapter 4. Corporate Governance and Risk Management — 11

Lesson: James Lam, Enterprise Risk Management: *From Incentives to Controls*, 2nd Edition (Hoboken, NJ: John Wiley & Sons, 2014). Chapter 4. What Is ERM? — 13

Lesson: René Stulz, "Risk Management, Governance, Culture and Risk Taking in Banks," *FRBNY Economic Policy Review* (August 2016): 43–59 — 15

Lesson: Steve Allen, *Financial Risk Management: A Practitioner's Guide to Managing Market and Credit Risk*, 2nd Edition (Hoboken, NJ: John Wiley & Sons, 2013). Chapter 4. Financial Disasters — 19

Lesson: Markus K. Brunnermeier, "Deciphering the Liquidity and Credit Crunch 2007–2008," *Journal of Economic Perspectives* 23, no. 1 (2009): 77–100 — 23

Lesson: Gary Gorton and Andrew Metrick. "Getting Up to Speed on the Financial Crisis: A One-Weekend-Reader's Guide," *Journal of Economic Literature* 50, no. 1 (2012): 128–150 — 29

Lesson: "René Stulz, "Risk Management Failures: What Are They and When Do They Happen?" Fisher College of Business Working Paper Series, October 2008 — 33

Lesson: "Edwin J. Elton, Martin J. Gruber, Stephen J. Brown and William N. Goetzmann, *Modern Portfolio Theory and Investment Analysis*, 9th Edition (Hoboken, NJ: John Wiley & Sons, 2014). Chapter 13. The Standard Capital Asset Pricing Model — 37

© 2017 Wiley

Lesson: Noel Amenc and Veronique Le Sourd, *Portfolio Theory and Performance Analysis* (West Sussex, England: John Wiley & Sons, 2003). Chapter 4. Applying the CAPM to Performance Measurement: Single-Index Performance Measurement Indicators (Section 4.2 only) — 41

Lesson: Zvi Bodie, Alex Kane, and Alan J. Marcus, *Investments*, 10th Edition (New York: McGraw-Hill, 2013). Chapter 10. Arbitrage Pricing Theory and Multifactor Models of Risk and Return — 45

Lesson: "Principles for Effective Data Aggregation and Risk Reporting," (Basel Committee on Banking Supervision Publication, January 2013) — 51

Lesson: GARP Code of Conduct — 55

Quantitative Analysis

Lesson: Michael Miller, *Mathematics and Statistics for Financial Risk Management*, 2nd Edition (Hoboken, NJ: John Wiley & Sons, 2013). Chapter 2. Probabilities — 61

Lesson: Michael Miller, *Mathematics and Statistics for Financial Risk Management*, 2nd Edition (Hoboken, NJ: John Wiley & Sons, 2013). Chapter 3. Basic Statistics — 67

Lesson: Michael Miller, *Mathematics and Statistics for Financial Risk Management*, 2nd Edition (Hoboken, NJ: John Wiley & Sons, 2013). Chapter 4. Distributions — 75

Lesson: Michael Miller, *Mathematics and Statistics for Financial Risk Management*, 2nd Edition (Hoboken, NJ: John Wiley & Sons, 2013). Chapter 6. Bayesian Analysis (pp. 113–124 only) — 83

Lesson: Michael Miller, *Mathematics and Statistics for Financial Risk Management*, 2nd Edition (Hoboken, NJ: John Wiley & Sons, 2013). Chapter 7. Hypothesis Testing and Confidence Intervals — 87

Lesson: James Stock and Mark Watson, *Introduction to Econometrics*, Brief Edition (Boston: Pearson Education, 2008). Chapter 4. Linear Regression with One Regressor — 99

Lesson: James Stock and Mark Watson, *Introduction to Econometrics*, Brief Edition (Boston: Pearson Education, 2008). Chapter 5. Regression with a Single Regressor — 113

Lesson: James Stock and Mark Watson, *Introduction to Econometrics*, Brief Edition (Boston: Pearson Education, 2008). Chapter 6. Linear Regression with Multiple Regressors — 119

Lesson: James Stock and Mark Watson, *Introduction to Econometrics*, Brief Edition (Boston: Pearson Education, 2008). Chapter 7. Hypothesis Tests and Confidence Intervals in Multiple Regression — 127

Lesson: Francis X. Diebold, *Elements of Forecasting*, 4th Edition (Mason, Ohio: Cengage Learning, 2006). Chapter 5. Modeling and Forecasting Trend — 135

Lesson: Francis X. Diebold, *Elements of Forecasting*, 4th Edition (Mason, Ohio: Cengage Learning, 2006). Chapter 6. Modeling and Forecasting Seasonality — 141

Lesson: Francis X. Diebold, *Elements of Forecasting*, 4th Edition (Mason, Ohio: Cengage Learning, 2006). Chapter 7. Characterizing Cycles — 143

Lesson: Francis X. Diebold, *Elements of Forecasting*, 4th Edition (Mason, Ohio: Cengage Learning, 2006). Chapter 8. Modeling Cycles: MA, AR, and ARMA Models — 149

Lesson: John C. Hull, *Risk Management and Financial Institutions*, 4th Edition (Hoboken, NJ: John Wiley & Sons, 2015). Chapter 10. Volatility — 153

Lesson: John Hull, *Risk Management and Financial Institutions*, 4th Edition (Hoboken, NJ: John Wiley & Sons, 2015). Chapter 11. Correlations and Copulas — 159

Lesson: Chris Brooks, *Introductory Econometrics for Finance*, 3rd Edition (Cambridge, UK: Cambridge University Press, 2014). Chapter 13. Simulation Methods — 163

How to Study for the Exam

The FRM Exam Part I curriculum covers the tools used to assess financial risk:

- Foundations of risk management—20%
- Quantitative analysis—20%
- Financial markets and products—30%
- Valuation and risk models—30%

It is important to focus only on the learning objectives as you are asked about them and pay close attention to the percentages of each section. That is the core of my focus throughout the text, the online lecture sessions, and with the practice questions. A study hour doesn't count unless you are laser focused on specifically how GARP asks a learning objective.

Consistency is also key. Making a regular weekly study time is going to be important to staying on track. There is a reason: Only ~50% of the candidates pass the exam every year. It's a tough exam. It also tests intuition, not just memorization. That is why I attempt at every opportunity to connect the dots across readings, teach how changing environments change both markets and the models we use to model them, as well as help you with the questions where GARP specifically wants you to calculate an outcome.

Calculator policy:

It is best to begin your study with one of the approved calculators. You will not be admitted to the exam without one of these approved calculators!

- Hewlett Packard 12C (including the HP 12C Platinum and the Anniversary Edition)
- Hewlett Packard 10B II
- Hewlett Packard 10B II+
- Hewlett Packard 20B
- Texas Instruments BA II Plus (including the BA II Plus Professional)

Every year, candidates are turned away from the exam site because of wrong calculators. Make sure you aren't one of them.

ABOUT THE INSTRUCTOR

Christian H. Cooper is an author and trader based in New York City. He initially created the FRM program because, as a candidate, he was frustrated with the quality of study programs available. Writing from a practitioner's point of view, Christian drew on his experience as a trader across fixed income and equity markets, most recently as head of derivatives trading at a bank in New York, to create a program that is very focused on exam results while connecting the dots across topics to increase intuition and understanding.

Christian is active with the Aspen Institute; he is a Truman National Security Fellow, and a term member at the Council on Foreign Relations.

Wiley FRM Exam Review Study Guide 2017
Part I, Volume 1

FOUNDATIONS OF RISK MANAGEMENT (FRM)

This area focuses on your knowledge of foundational concepts of risk management and how risk management can add value to an organization. The broad areas of knowledge covered in foundations-related readings include the following:

- Basic risk types, measurement and management tools
- Creating value with risk management
- The role of risk management in corporate governance
- Enterprise risk management (ERM)
- Financial disasters and risk management failures
- The Capital Asset Pricing Model (CAPM)
- Risk-adjusted performance measurement
- Multi-factor models
- Information risk and data quality management
- Ethics and the GARP Code of Conduct

Crouhy, Chapter 1

Michel Crouhy, Dan Galai, and Robert Mark, *The Essentials of Risk Management*, 2nd Edition (New York: McGraw-Hill, 2014). Chapter 1. Risk Management: A Helicopter View (Including Appendix 1.1)

After completing this reading you should be able to:

- Explain the concept of risk and compare risk management with risk taking.
- Describe the risk management process and identify problems and challenges which can arise in the risk management process.
- Evaluate and apply tools and procedures used to measure and manage risk, including quantitative measures, qualitative assessment, and enterprise risk management.
- Distinguish between expected loss and unexpected loss, and provide examples of each.
- Interpret the relationship between risk and reward and explain how conflicts of interest can impact risk management.
- Describe and differentiate between the key classes of risks, explain how each type of risk can arise, and assess the potential impact of each type of risk on an organization.

Learning objective: Explain the concept of risk and compare risk management with risk taking.

Within the context of the FRM exam, risk is defined as variability of outcomes. These outcomes can be the result of a wide array of changes in expected future cash flows (earning potential), a change in book value (balance sheet assets), or broader economic variables. Companies are often exposed to an incredibly diverse range of risks, which could be described as business or financial risks.

Business risks include decisions purely related to business development, including marketing decisions, new product development, etc. Financial risks are risks that occur from changes in interest rates or other market movements. Ideally, companies will work to identify and minimize financial risks so they can concentrate on the risk to their business. A core concept of risk management is how a good business can be destroyed by mismanaged financial risks.

Learning objective: Describe the risk management process and identify problems and challenges which can arise in the risk management process.

The risk management process begins with identifying risk exposures, quantifying those exposures if possible, determining to keep or hedge the risk, finding the appropriate way to mitigate the risk if that is the choice—selling a business line or using financial products to hedge the risk are all ways of mitigating.

The big takeaway from this reading is this: Something may not be considered risk by the model or the market until something goes wrong. Risk management helps us monitor known risks but it is not so great at finding or predicting new sources of risk.

> **Learning objective: Evaluate and apply tools and procedures used to measure and manage risk, including quantitative measures, qualitative assessment, and enterprise risk management.**

There are a number of quantitative and qualitative tools you need to know for the exam. Right now, just focus on these:

Stop Loss—Stop loss means "stop my losses at this price." For example, if you are long a stock and you enter a stop-loss order, you are entering an order to exit the trade actually below where the current market is trading. To make this more concrete, if you own a stock at $50 and you wish to stop your losses at $45, your stop-loss order would be entered with a limit of $45. The problem with stop-loss orders is that they usually can trade through your limit leaving the order unexecuted. In other words, a stop-loss order is not a guarantee that you will exit the trade at the price that you want.

For purposes of risk management, this means that you could be open to larger losses than the stop price of your order, and that is what you need to know for the exam.

Notional Limits—Notional limits refer to the absolute dollar value that is committed to a trade. It has been an ineffective method of risk management.

There are limits to the use of notionals, however, because they only consider the dollar value committed to the trade. For example, a $1 billion trade in a bond with a duration of one year has significantly less risk than a single $1 billion investment in a 30-year bond—which has a much longer duration and therefore much higher risk for the same notional amount. Therefore, risk management by controlling notional amounts of derivatives, cash, or securities is ineffective because it does not put risk limits in terms of risk but in terms of notional, which is not an effective measure of risk. No major firm will look at risk in this way.

Scenario Analysis—Scenario analysis can be broadly lumped into a method of risk management that re-prices a portfolio over a wide range of outcomes. Scenario analysis typically takes a predefined scenario and alters the portfolio value (PV) according to that historical outcome. For example, if we again lose 23% of the stock market's value in a single day (as we did on Black Monday), then what effect would there be on our portfolio?

Stress Tests—The key difference between scenario analysis and a stress test is usually the range of potential outcomes. For example, stress tests can be used to test a portfolio to the limit of what would normally be expected under extreme events—including correlation going to one, and the normal inverse relationship between stocks and bonds breaking down.

Duration and Beta Exposure Limits—Duration and beta exposure limits are, on the surface, a better measure of risk control than notional limits, stop-loss limits, or stress test and scenario analysis. The reason is that beta refers to the variation expected within an equity portfolio, and duration is a measure of fixed-income risk. For example, an equity portfolio with a beta of 1.25 would, on average, be expected to have a variation 1.25 times greater than the underlying equity portfolio. Duration, on the other hand, is a measure of how long it takes to get your return of principal invested in a particular bond. The longer the duration, the greater the risk of the bond.

VaR—Value at risk is among the most widely used measures of risk because of its ease and simplicity. However, the ease of use belies the complex assumptions that the model makes. Due to the complexity of the underlying assumptions, VaR is often misused and/or misunderstood. While the mathematics of VaR are completely sound, the complexity of the VaR assumes a high degree of understanding about the assumptions of the model, which include how asset prices behave.

Learning objective: Distinguish between expected loss and unexpected loss, and provide examples of each.

Think of expected losses as when the market moves and you actually lose as much as you expected. This is a good thing because it means your risk runs are right and everything is working as it should. The problem arises when you actually lose more than you expected. It is equally as problematic when you lose less than you expected because it means something is wrong with your data, your calibration, or your model. So-called "tying out" is the single most important thing a desk can do—even more than generating a profit. If a desk doesn't tie out it means something is wrong and this is the biggest micro risk flag an institution can face. Unexpected losses, or unexpected gains, all merit extra scrutiny.

Learning objective: Interpret the relationship between risk and reward and explain how conflicts of interest can impact risk management.

The greater the risk, the greater the potential for reward. We will come back to this more in the CAPM section where we quantify risk and portfolio construction. We will discuss a number of types of risk and you should know these definitions early on:

Market Risk—Risk that stems from changes in market prices or changes in the variability of market prices. The author highlights two types of market risk. *Absolute market risk* is used to measure the change in a portfolio's value in dollar terms. *Relative risk*, by contrast, is used to measure the change in a portfolio according to some benchmark. An example of relative market risk would be the use of beta to limit or describe potential changes in equity portfolio relative to its underlying index.

Liquidity Risk—There are two types of liquidity risk you need to know. *Market/product liquidity* is the risk of moving the market due to the size of the trade necessary to manage risks. This type of risk is usually product-type specific. Secondly, there is *inability to meet cash flow requirements*, which could be an inability to pay on swaps or a pension fund unable to meet obligations. It can take many forms, related to any cash flow operation necessary for continued business operation.

Credit Risk—Credit risk seeks to describe the probability of counterparty failure. In this case, the risk manager wants to evaluate the probability that a counterparty is either unwilling or unable to meet their financial obligations.

An example is if a sovereign state declared all foreign liability null and void. In this case, the counterparty, the sovereign state, is perhaps able to make interest payments but is unwilling to do so.

By contrast, the more common example of credit risk is when a company is unable to meet its interest payment obligations.

Operational Risk—Operational risk is perhaps the most qualitative of all types of risk. Generically, operational risk describes the possibility of a breakdown in processes, the breakdown of a model, or the risk of fraud.

> **Learning objective: Describe and differentiate between the key classes of risks, explain how each type of risk can arise, and assess the potential impact of each type of risk on an organization.**

Market Risk—This is the general risk of a change in asset prices due to a change in the overall market. This can refer to any type of market not just the listed stock market. Even commodity markets can have market risk and this is distinct from commodity risk which we will see in a moment. Also you will see general market risk discussed in the Capital Asset Pricing Model when we see this is effectively the risk that cannot be diversified away in a portfolio.

Interest Rate Risk—Changes in interest rate risk will impact different assets in different ways. For bonds and swaps, of course, there is the direct impact of change in the yield curve but for futures it could impact the cost of carry or time value of money—almost an inconsequential change. On the exam you will see bonds with embedded options and we will see how just having an option on the bond changes the degree to which interest rates change asset values.

Equity Price Risk—This is the risk of a portfolio that can be diversified away—the individual stock specific risk of a particular company. This will come up often in portfolio theory.

Foreign Exchange Risk—Unless there is direct exposure to foreign exchange through reserves or futures contracts, foreign exchange risk impacts companies indirectly. When a domestic currency rises relative to a foreign currency, this makes domestic goods more expensive and therefore less competitive, which may dampen a company's future income potential and weigh down the stock as investors weight the changes in the global FX markets.

Commodity Price Risk—There are a few unique characteristics of commodity risk. First, there is usually a concentrated supply among a few large market players so liquidity risk can become a factor. Consequently, commodities often have greater volatility than other assets. Also, for some commodities there are risks that are effectively un-hedgeable (weather for instance), although there is a market for weather futures, which is only an indirect hedge at best. Also for commodities that are perishable or have high storage costs, their spot and futures prices may behave in odd ways, which we will discuss later.

Credit Risk—There are really only two ways credit risk is realized: (1) when a counter-party actually fails to fulfill obligations and cannot pay, which results in bankruptcy proceedings, or (2) when the possibility of failure to pay becomes priced into the marketplace and corporate bonds or credit default swaps change in price in response to some credit event.

Portfolio Credit Risk—This type of risk looks at the exposure an institution may have to particular industrial sectors or at particular times. If a bank has a large exposure to the automobile industry and we experience an economic recession then that bank will certainly have risks at the portfolio level, not just at individual companies.

Liquidity Risk—This is a big issue on the FRM exam because this usually occurs in times of stress when everyone is trying to get out of a particular asset class at the same time—or cover short sales—and there is a lack of liquidity to fulfill orders so the market price is moved based on the amount of volume going "one way."

Operational Risk—We will spend a lot of time on operational risk (especially in Part Two) because it is so broad and subjective. It is the risk that a business operation fails and has a market impact on its supply chain or capacity to stay in business. There are five basic types:
1. *Legal and regulatory risk*—The risk that a company fails to comply with a known or unknown regulation or law and the economic consequence of that failure be it fines or perhaps the loss of a license to conduct business.
2. *Business risk*—This is risk of poor management decisions, bad products, poor supply chain management, inventory, etc. Everything governing the production and management of a business falls under this type of operational risk.
3. *Strategic risk*—Strategic risk is the possibility for large investments with high payoff potential to fail. Any company deciding to enter a new market is an example of strategic risk.
4. *Reputation risk*—This is the risk of a change in reputation that has the capacity to reduce the company's prospect to exist as a going concern in the future. Does a seemingly minor issue now lead to longer term negative consequences?
5. *Systemic risk*—Don't be confused by "systemic" versus "systematic." This type, systemic, is the chance the failure of one company starts a chain reaction and brings the entire "system" down, hence the name. We will discuss systemic risk in portfolio management—the risk a portfolio has to a particular stock or asset that usually can be diversified away.

Crouhy, Chapter 2

Michel Crouhy, Dan Galai, and Robert Mark, *The Essentials of Risk Management*, 2nd Edition (New York: McGraw-Hill, 2014). Chapter 2. Corporate Risk Management: A Primer

After completing this reading you should be able to:

- Evaluate some advantages and disadvantages of hedging risk exposures.
- Explain considerations and procedures in determining a firm's risk appetite and its business objectives.
- Explain how a company can determine whether to hedge specific risk factors, including the role of the board of directors and the process of mapping risks.
- Apply appropriate methods to hedge operational and financial risks, including pricing, foreign currency, and interest rate risk.
- Assess the impact of risk management instruments.

Learning objective: Evaluate some advantages and disadvantages of hedging risk exposures.

Learning objective: Explain considerations and procedures in determining a firm's risk appetite and its business objectives.

This is a low probability for the exam but know that companies typically want to hedge "non-core" risks to their business. For example, Ford Credit Services has huge interest rate risks and they can use a range of products to hedge them. Hedging has costs and prevents profitability based on financial market price movements. Hedging risk removes uncertainty and reduces potential profitability on market moves but leaving risks unhedged opens the company to potential losses from non-core areas (changes in financial price levels). Each company will have different policies governing this risk management style at an enterprise level.

Learning objective: Explain how a company can determine whether to hedge specific risk factors, including the role of the board of directors and the process of mapping risks.

With all financial risks, the board needs to consider absolute, relative, or basis risk types within the type of risk. For example, interest rate risk potentially has relative, absolute, and basis risk types.

Understand these terms:

Absolute: In pure dollar terms

Relative: To a benchmark

Basis Risk: A risk exposure to the relative change in valuation between two similar asset classes with similar risk profiles. A good example is owning 10-year Treasuries and paying on 10-year swap rates. Both assets have similar risk profiles in terms of duration but have different credit risks with different market participants in each class. Another example is trading spot currencies versus futures or cash bonds versus the corresponding futures contract.

Nondirectional Market Risk: Is not dependent on the direction of the underlying assets. Normally it refers to the change between assets such as basis risks.

Learning objective: Apply appropriate methods to hedge operational and financial risks, including pricing, foreign currency, and interest rate risk.

The operational risks a company can face, especially an international company when they have licensing, borrowing, acquisitions, and cash flows in multiple currencies, can significantly impact their financial standing.

Plus, it is very difficult to predict with a degree of high precision how much of a foreign currency hedge you need when you don't know exactly how much in overseas sales any company may have.

Here is the way to address all of these:

1. Hedge in "layers"—Hedge known foreign revenues that can be forecast exactly and add additional hedges on as sales grow.
2. Manage the value of balance sheet assets denominated in other assets with foreign currency forwards. Negative changes in the balance sheet reduce shareholder equity directly, so this is especially important.
3. Use interest rate swaps to manage the net exposure to interest rate risks.

Learning objective: Assess the impact of risk management instruments.

When GARP refers to "risk management instruments," they are talking about the futures, options, and swaps that can be used to hedge the risks of a portfolio or company. Within the context of a corporation, GARP wants you to know a risk management strategy that loses money isn't necessarily an example of poor risk management (although that can happen), but rather if a hedging strategy has a negative impact on the performance of the company, that is simply the cost of hedging that risk and is not a poor reflection on risk management. Now, this does not mean that risk management strategies that are wrong due to model or trader error are not legitimate errors. It means that the impact from risk management can have a positive or negative profit and loss even when correctly applied.

CROUHY, CHAPTER 4

Michel Crouhy, Dan Galai, and Robert Mark, The Essentials of Risk Management, 2nd Edition (New York: McGraw-Hill, 2014). Chapter 4. Corporate Governance and Risk Management

After completing this reading you should be able to:

- Compare and contrast best practices in corporate governance with those of risk management.
- Assess the role and responsibilities of the board of directors in risk governance.
- Evaluate the relationship between a firm's risk appetite and its business strategy, including the role of incentives.
- Distinguish the different mechanisms for transmitting risk governance throughout an organization.
- Illustrate the interdependence of functional units within a firm as it relates to risk management.
- Assess the role and responsibilities of a firm's audit committee.

Learning objective: Compare and contrast best practices in corporate governance with those of risk management.

One big issue on the FRM exam is the idea of *agency risk*. This means large risks that are taken by a party who will have little to no share of the downside risk if the trade goes bad.

For example, companies that are having cash flow problems may face credit downgrades which raise their borrowing costs in the open market. This in turn forces that company to take on projects that are riskier to cover the higher cost of capital. A manager, in an attempt to protect their job, may risks hundreds of millions on risky projects or trades—an extreme example—in an attempt to turn the company around but will share in only a fraction of the losses (losing a job) if the idea doesn't work out.

Corporate governance is the attempt to reduce agency risk within a company by formulating policies and procedures at the board level that protect the long-term interest of the shareholders, avoid taking outsized risks that put the company at risk, and ensure the long-term survivability of the firm.

Learning objective: Assess the role and responsibilities of the board of directors in risk governance.

The board's largest role is being independent, defining a risk appetite in line with a company's capacity and willingness to take risk, ensuring that an effective risk management program is in place to ensure compliance with risk limits, and mitigating the risks the board deems unsuitable.

This reading goes into quite a bit of detail about how a board of directors can manage risk but in reality all of these occur at a very high level and it isn't the board's responsibility to manage businesses, but rather it is to hold managers accountable to the stated risk limits of the company.

Learning objective: Evaluate the relationship between a firm's risk appetite and its business strategy, including the role of incentives.

This is fairly straightforward in the readings and GARP seems to want to highlight that there are risks that arise during the normal course of a business that, even though they occur normally within the business strategy, are inconsistent with the firm's risk appetite. For example, an automobile company that also has a lending arm to finance the sale of its vehicles would not want to take large amounts of interest rate risk even though that risk arises from a part of this normal course of business. That makes this risk, the interest rate risk of its loans, a good candidate for hedging or selling.

Learning objective: Distinguish the different mechanisms for transmitting risk governance throughout an organization.

Risk limits are usually set top down at the risk committee level and then distributed among the different business lines. Depending on the type of business, this can be either a VaR limit or a capital allocation. We speak about both VaR limits and economic capital in later readings but know for now this is almost universally a top-down approach.

Learning objective: Illustrate the interdependence of functional units within a firm as it relates to risk management.

In this example, the risk management interdependence relates to an investment bank and the market risk it is taking.

Probably the single most important idea I have learned on the trading floor with respect to risk management is to pay attention to the unexplained profits and losses. If there is extra money, either more or less, there is either model risk, bad data, poor calibration, or other factors. Anything could be wrong and that is the best way to monitor for problems within the trading book.

That idea of trading informing operations or the quantitative groups that something is wrong is an example of this interdependence. The idea here is that nothing within a trading floor operates in a vacuum.

Learning objective: Assess the role and responsibilities of a firm's audit committee.

This is a low priority for the exam, but know that the audit committee is the way the board can independently verify that what is being reported to the board with respect to risk management is actually accurate. It would be counterproductive to let trading operations self-report its own risk with no independent verification, so the audit committee ensures compliance from a regulatory point of view and ensures compliance with the firm's own stated policies with respect to risk management.

Lam, Chapter 4

James Lam, *Enterprise Risk Management: From Incentives to Controls*, 2nd Edition (Hoboken, NJ: John Wiley & Sons, 2014). Chapter 4. What Is ERM?

After completing this reading you should be able to:

- Describe enterprise risk management (ERM) and compare and contrast differing definitions of ERM.
- Compare the benefits and costs of ERM and describe the motivations for a firm to adopt an ERM initiative.
- Describe the role and responsibilities of the chief risk officer (CRO) and assess how the CRO should interact with other senior management.
- Distinguish between components of an ERM program.

Learning objective: Describe enterprise risk management (ERM) and compare and contrast differing definitions of ERM.

The intent of ERM is to identify, manage, hedge, and control risks across the entire firm. Since ERM includes topics such as operation and supply chain risks, there are more qualitative elements that extend beyond a simplistic Capital Asset Pricing Model (CAPM)—which we will discuss in portfolio management—or the cost-of-capital method of accounting for firm-level risks.

Beyond the risks the firm explicitly faces, ERM also includes the estimation of potential risks, the likelihood those events will occur, and the corresponding losses. Many of these areas are highly subjective and are inputs into other analysis so there is the risk for garbage in–garbage out with respect to enterprise risk management.

Learning objective: Compare the benefits and costs of ERM and describe the motivations for a firm to adopt an ERM initiative.

You can ignore the costs part of this question and focus on the benefits. The reason is that various costs are too varied from company to company to be included on the exam. As for the benefits of ERM, the motivation is usually preservation of shareholder value.

In an increasingly connected economy, firms can have risk exposures that go beyond simple changes in sales and a qualitative ERM approach allows senior management the space to consider "what if" scenarios outside of a simple quantitative model that assigns VaR to a portfolio of assets.

Learning objective: Describe the role and responsibilities of the chief risk officer (CRO) and assess how the CRO should interact with other senior management.

The chief risk officer reports to the board of directors and is the principal officer that determines the risk levels taken, the models and methods used to asses risk, and is usually the first line of defense for senior leadership to be briefed on emerging risks a company may face and their potential consequences.

Learning objective: Distinguish between components of an ERM program.

For the exam, know there are four parts to an ERM program:

1. Define a risk policy for the firm. This includes developing lists of risks the enterprise faces, the methods, both qualitative and quantitative, those risks will be assessed, set up a framework of potential impact of a risk event by estimating the potential change in cash flows.
2. Estimate as accurately as possible the risks the company faces. In some cases, ERM attempts to apply quantitative measures to things such as operational risk, but when probabilities are associated with high-impact, low-probability events, it is difficult to include that risk in a meaningful way with a VaR analysis. For the exam, know that ERM and VaR both have their own shortcomings.
3. Compare the risk estimates faced by a firm and decide if the company should avoid them, transfer them to another party, reduce them through hedging, or keep the risk as a normal part of business.
4. Monitor the risk profile and performance. You will hear me emphasize this again and again. The most important element of managing risk on a desk, or at the enterprise level, is to match expected returns to the level of risk taken. This is why we will move into expected portfolio returns and the Capital Asset Pricing Model in the next few sections.

Stulz, FRBNY Economic Policy Review

René Stulz, "Risk Management, Governance, Culture and Risk Taking in Banks,"
FRBNY Economic Policy Review (August 2016): 43–59

After completing this reading you should be able to:

- Assess methods that banks can use to determine their optimal level of risk exposure, and explain how the optimal level of risk can differ across banks.
- Describe implications for a bank if it takes too little or too much risk compared to its optimal level.
- Explain ways in which risk management can add or destroy value for a bank.
- Describe structural challenges and limitations to effective risk management, including the use of VaR in setting limits.
- Assess the potential impact of a bank's governance, incentive structure, and risk culture on its risk profile and its performance.

Learning objective: Assess methods that banks can use to determine their optimal level of risk exposure, and explain how the optimal level of risk can differ across banks.

The focus here is the tension between a bank's equity and its leverage. Finding the initial balance is difficult enough, but there is also a feedback loop when banks get into trouble. A bank's value is a function of its future discounted cash flows and the discounted value of the cost of financial stress, meaning higher costs of capital, more defaults, and so on. This in turn could push the firm to reduce risk, lower returns, and increase the probability a bank will be unable to stay solvent and therefore increase the cost of future financial stress.

That is in theory, anyway.

In reality, banks generate profits from both assets and liabilities, and the leverage of a bank plays a key role in managing overall risk. This optimal level is the balance of leverage just before the tipping point of the negative feedback loop of higher funding costs, higher credit losses, management being forced to take less risk, the market pricing in future losses, and repeat until insolvent.

There is also a point reached where the incremental risk taken increases the potential losses beyond the gain of the new risk. This could also be defined as the optimal amount of risk, and it varies widely from institution to institution.

The operational concern here is that, in a decentralized environment in which incremental changes in risk/return aren't available in real time, this is increasingly difficult to manage and/or implement. In reality, there has to be a better way to determine what the optimal level of risk actually is.

The way to determine the optimal level of risk is to first determine the risk appetite, which will also differ from firm to firm.

Incidentally, the working paper argues the "right" credit rating is somewhere around the single A credit rating, because pursuing a rating higher than that implies that the bank is giving up many risky projects it could otherwise undertake.

Also, the rating that maximizes value across banks will depend on the nature of the banking business itself. A bank that has a large balance sheet of long-term over-the-counter (OTC) swap obligations may need a higher credit rating because of the credit service agreements it has in place against those existing bilateral agreements. A bank that is more transactional is going to have less concern about its credit rating to a point. Again, this is the ambiguity around the optimal risk and how that level can differ across institutions.

Learning objective: Describe implications for a bank if it takes too little or too much risk compared to its optimal level.

All you need to know for the exam here is that there is a theoretical, optimal level of risk for a banking institution that differs from a nonfinancial institution because banks can generate revenue from both assets and liabilities. Therefore, leverage is a key component of this assessment. Also know that the disadvantages are asymmetric: **taking too much** risk can destroy value, but knowingly **taking too much,** however defined, has far worse outcomes. This is a low-probability subject for the test as it is kind of a difficult topic to test.

Learning objective: Explain ways in which risk management can add or destroy value for a bank.

Risk management can actually destroy value in a number of ways. Risk managers can destroy value by not making sure the bank has the right amount of risk for the type of business and capital structure the bank has. Having too little risk is almost as bad as having too much risk in terms of value creation and preservation.

There are lots of ways this can happen. Banks can mismeasure bad risks so the bank actually has too much risk when risk management thought it was optimal. Total portfolio risk can fail to accommodate the opportunity costs of taking on new risk. A new project or loan may have an incremental value at risk (VaR) increase less than the potential profit, but how does that incremental change in the portfolio impact the capacity to take on future risk at potentially lower costs?

Also, if the risk management regime becomes too inflexible to adapt to new conditions or allow for new projects when available, the bank can drift away from what was previously an optimal hedge but now is inefficient for the shareholders.

For the exam, know that "too little risk" or "too much risk" can also be miscalculated, and that is just as damaging as knowingly taking on too little or too much risk.

Learning objective: Describe structural challenges and limitations to effective risk management, including the use of VaR in setting limits.

One key challenge is cultural. Risk management is rarely seen as a partner in value creation and is instead seen only as a Basel III–mandated policeman. That is the key structural challenge. The other structural challenge is how independent are the risk management functions and the business functions.

Completely eliminating mobility between the front and the middle/back offices not only limits the talent pool to draw from but also ensures that few will be interested in those roles if no mobility is allowed.

If there is some mobility, the risk management function could be influenced by the relationship the risk managers have with the risk takers. The reading doesn't propose solutions to these structural changes, but you should be aware that the independence of the risk management function is paramount but it is unclear how to enforce this independence.

In addition to the daily risk management that an institution may undertake to manage the day-to-day risk, the enterprise-level risk management focuses on catastrophic losses—losses that put the existence of the firm at risk. To do this, the economic capital of the firm (the capital necessary to exist as a going concern) must be known and targeted with some defined probability. This is obviously a perfect task for VaR.

The problems with setting limits with VaR are many and start with the limitations of VaR itself. Another issue is the granularity at which VaR is calculated. Obviously, a bank's value at risk is not the sum total of its VaR numbers. A trader who can enter and exit positions rapidly may trade at maximum VaR all the time, but a profitable unit in a different business that contributes to VaR may operate at under the maximum VaR just to keep some capacity to take risks.

Bottom line: Using VaR to set limits across business lines has as many limitations as the number and types of business lines themselves.

Learning objective: Assess the potential impact of a bank's governance, incentive structure, and risk culture on its risk profile and its performance.

This entire reading is about treating the risk management process, and the technology behind it, akin to the manufacturing technology of the industrial revolution. Banks exist to take risks, and a bank that is consistently below its optimum risk profile will struggle to create wealth for its shareholders. The question here is: How do we use incentives and corporate culture in the right way?

This is a more important question than it might seem at the surface. The cultural divide between the front and back offices has immense cost, both within and without the financial system. That culture is often rooted in knowledge or the lack thereof. Trading desks often see back- and middle-office functions as only cost centers that serve no real function. This is clearly not the case. The bottom line here is that banks need to use compensation incentives and promote a culture in which risk management is a partner in creating value, not just a consumer of value.

Allen, Chapter 4

Steve Allen, *Financial Risk Management: A Practitioner's Guide to Managing Market and Credit Risk*, 2nd Edition (Hoboken, NJ: John Wiley & Sons, 2013).
Chapter 4. Financial Disasters

After completing this reading you should be able to:

- Analyze the key factors that led to and derive the lessons learned from the following risk management case studies:
    - Chase Manhattan and its involvement with Drysdale Securities
    - Kidder Peabody
    - Barings
    - Allied Irish Bank
    - Union Bank of Switzerland (UBS)
    - Société Générale
    - Long Term Capital Management (LTCM)
    - Metallgesellschaft
    - Bankers Trust
    - JPMorgan, Citigroup, and Enron

Learning objective: Analyze the key factors that led to and derive the lessons learned from the following risk management case studies:

- Chase Manhattan and its involvement with Drysdale Securities
- Kidder Peabody
- Barings
- Allied Irish Bank
- Union Bank of Switzerland (UBS)
- Société Générale
- Long Term Capital Management (LTCM)
- Metallgesellschaft
- Bankers Trust
- JPMorgan, Citigroup, and Enron

CHASE MANHATTAN AND ITS INVOLVEMENT WITH DRYSDALE SECURITIES

This event occurred in 1976 and centered on unsecured lending on the part of Drysdale that took advantage of a system error. This borrowed capital was used to take market positions and when this capital was lost, the firm (Drysdale) went bust.

Lessons learned: After the failure of Drysdale, industry-wide controls were put into place to make the collateral calculation of borrowing accurate.

KIDDER PEABODY

Kidder Peabody's loss was rooted in the erroneous reporting of $350M in profits from a single trader. The large profit and loss (P&L) attributed to a single trader led to a wide investigation of his activity.

Lessons learned: Always explain PNL in terms of risk being taken and investigate any unusual gains. There is truly no free lunch.

BARINGS

Over the course of two years, a new trader sent by Barings Bank to Singapore to develop their futures business there lost over $1 billion making unauthorized trades. The amazing part of this story is the first trade wasn't actually fraudulent—it was a trading error! Being new and not wanting to report the loss, Nick Leeson created an error account and began to take positions in futures to make up the loss, which snowballed into a loss that wiped out the entire equity of the bank.

Lessons learned: From a risk management perspective it is critical to maintain a back office that is independent of trading and willing to raise questions when necessary.

ALLIED IRISH BANK

Again, this financial disaster involved a single trader and massive unauthorized positions. This carried on for five years and netted $691 million in losses.

Lessons learned: As in the Barings' financial disaster: Decompose PNL in terms of risk taken, create an independent back office, and implement systems controls that limit the ability to book trades off the books.

UNION BANK OF SWITZERLAND (UBS)

The UBS loss of 1997 was not a single event but a collection of events that resulted from poor oversight. Furthermore, after the 1997 losses were uncovered, UBS was forced into a merger with Swiss Bank Corporation. UBS had made a significant investment in Long Term Capital Management and seems not to have disclosed the risk or size of that investment which resulted in another $800 million dollar loss in 1998 when LTCM went broke.

In 1997, UBS had long dated options whose valuation was impacted by changes in British law, unhedged Japanese warrants on bank stock, an overly optimistic valuation on exotic equity option baskets, and losses related to model error. In addition, the risk management head was also the head of quantitative analytics that was responsible for pricing the exotic instruments and whose compensation was tied to trading profits.

Lessons learned: Two things: UBS had trades on that they weren't monitoring or valuing properly and even if they were, there was a senior risk manager who had two hats on—the risk management side and the trading side. This was a significant breach of best practices.

SOCIÉTÉ GÉNÉRALE

This disaster came to light early in 2008 when a junior trader who had previously worked in the middle office lost over $7 billion taking unauthorized positions.

Apparently the fraud began in the summer of 2005 and the trader was able to conceal the massive losses by entering fake, offsetting trades into the risk management system that had a forward starting date. Knowing the middle office would not check the trade with the counterparty until the starting date approached, he was able to book, then cancel forward starting trades with values that offset his losses with no one ever checking.

Lessons learned: As with many of these losses attributed to a single individual, the failure came from a lack of oversight, no distinction between the trading floor and operations, inadequate supervision, and no consistent P&L generation. This trader was consistently reporting trading gains and that should immediately have raised a red flag. Furthermore, the trader never took a vacation so he was able to consistently cancel the forward trades and re-enter them—close to a thousand fraudulent trades—over and over. Most traders are required to take vacations and turn their books over to other traders.

LONG TERM CAPITAL MANAGEMENT (LTCM)

This failure was due not to fraud but to large market moves. LTCM was making large macro bets on volatility and correlation among assets which, when stressed, caused the historical relationships to break down. Since this failure wasn't due to fraud, it is more complex than previous examples.

Lessons learned: Reduce exposure to companies whose only source of revenue is trading. In other words, facing or having "real" companies to reduce counterparty risk since their performance is likely not directly correlated with financial asset performance.

Always include liquidity risk in the total risk of the position.

There must be broader adoption by the marketplace of positions. (This really didn't gain ground until the most recent crisis. Even so, centrally cleared swaps are only the tip of the iceberg.)

There must be wider adoption of stress testing in credit risk simulations. This helps to see what happens when counterparties begin to fail simply due to the failure of other institutions. This has obvious relevance to the 2007–2010 crisis.

METALLGESELLSCHAFT

GARP likes to ask about this one on the exam because it centers around one of their favorite topics: basis risk.

Metallgesellschaft (or MG) had long-term exposure to gas and oil prices because they were entering into private contracts with their customers as part of their normal business. The problem was these were long-term contracts with their customers and they were hedging this exposure with short-term futures contracts.

Lessons learned: Just because something is part of the "normal" course of business does not mean the firm can't be exposed to huge losses. This was not a speculative position but rather happened because the basis risk was not considered.

BANKERS TRUST

This is the infamous Procter & Gamble derivatives incident of the mid-1990s. A customer (Gibson Greetings) stated they were misled by Bankers Trust regarding the risks involved in a particular derivative trade.

Lessons learned: The biggest takeaway is to match the degree of the solution, or proposed solution, to the degree of the problem. Usually proposals that seem like a complex way to deal with a simple problem offer more degrees of freedom for the dealer to hide costs to the user that are normally obvious.

JPMORGAN, CITIGROUP, AND ENRON

The reason these are grouped together is that JPMorgan and Citigroup were the largest counterparties to Enron in the contracts they sold in the open market. It raised no suspicion for Enron to be heavily involved in selling oil contracts forward given their business model in the energy space. The issue was that the cash received from selling oil forward was booked as current income when, in fact, Enron had agreed to buy back the oil sold forward at a fixed price. Earnings were inflated by taking current income against future loans.

Lessons learned: Investment banks, like JPMorgan and Citigroup in this case, have access to information about what a particular customer is doing and are not immune from charges of fraud if they do nothing. To have a customer the size of Enron who did little except execute forward oil contracts should have raised red flags. Both banks agreed to pay a combined fine of $286 million for aiding in Enron's fraud.

Markus K. Brunnermeier, 2009. "Deciphering the Liquidity and Credit Crunch 2007–2008," *Journal of Economic Perspectives* 23:1, 77–100

After completing this reading, you should be able to:

- Describe the key factors that led to the housing bubble.
- Explain the banking industry trends leading up to the liquidity squeeze and assess the triggers for the liquidity crisis.
- Explain how banks created collateralized debt obligations.
- Explain the purposes and uses of credit default swaps.
- Describe how securitized and structured products were used by investor groups and describe the consequences of their increased use.
- Describe how the financial crisis triggered a series of worldwide financial and economic consequences.
- Distinguish between funding liquidity and market liquidity and explain how the evaporation of liquidity can lead to a financial crisis.
- Analyze how an increase in counterparty credit risk can generate additional funding needs and possible systemic risk.

Learning objective: Describe the key factors that led to the housing bubble.

First there was the environment of low-interest rates. The Fed saw no hint of a bubble or inflation and felt hesitant to raise rates after the implosion of the tech bubble of the late 1990s. There were immense capital inflows from abroad since rates were so cheap, and it was relatively cheap to buy dollars and defend their currencies in the open market at levels that were friendlier for exports. Probably the biggest change was the shift away from the motivation for securitization of assets. Traditional banks took credit risk and kept it on the balance sheet but the originate-to-distribute model replaced that model in which banks were motivated to purchase loans only with the intent of rebundling them and reselling them.

This originate-to-distribute model led to a decline in lending standards, and that was the real spiral that led to poor credit being enhanced with bad modeling and tranched risk being mispriced.

Learning objective: Explain the banking industry trends leading up to the liquidity squeeze and assess the triggers for the liquidity crisis.

There are two trends you really need to focus on. First was the large-scale move toward securitization and the originate-to-distribute model. Second, all these assets were financed with short-term commercial paper, which left banks particularly exposed to any liquidity shocks.

There were a few triggers leading up to the initial liquidity shocks. The creation of collateralized debt obligations (CDOs) and offloading of risk through securitization was certainly a path to liquidity squeeze, and when owners of tranches protected themselves by buying credit default swaps, there was some nasty feedback looks that created a real problem from a liquidity perspective.

Another trigger was shortening the duration of the maturity of the CDOs to fit the needs of the money market funds. Since rates were so low, money markets were looking for any lift increase in yield, and the securitized product space, if the maturity was short enough, could be bought by the trillion-dollar money market industry.

The problem with this idea is that short-maturity paper offers low yields. However, a bank could buy longer-term assets, hold them off the balance sheet, and sell notes against that collateral; this would fit the maturity cap of money market funds even though, technically, there was a much longer duration risk.

We also cannot overlook the importance of repo as a way for investment banks to finance their balance sheet with very short-term—sometimes overnight— borrowing to fund their balance sheets.

Despite the seemingly different nature of these problems, they are really all the same: a mismatch of maturity (borrowing short and paying long through either CDOs or off-balance-sheet holding companies).

Learning objective: Explain how banks created collateralized debt obligations.

There are a couple of steps to create a CDO. First, a bank will collect a diversified portfolio of mortgages and other types of loans like corporate debt or asset-backed loans. The portfolio is ordered in tranches that represent the credit quality of that "slice" of the portfolio, and these slices are sold to different investors who have different investor needs.

The problem really began when the assets in the tranches did not match the rating of the assets within that portion of the CDO.

Learning objective: Explain the purposes and uses of credit default swaps.

If buying a tranche of a CDO is going long an asset, you can think of a credit default swap as a hedge to selling that stock short. A CDS is explicitly an OTC contract insuring against a credit event of a bond or a tranche. These CDSs are like pay-fixed swaps in which there is a periodic payment in exchange for insurance on the underlying bond or tranche. The gross notional value of CDSs we are talking about is huge and probably on the order of $60 trillion.

One step beyond the CDS on a specific tranche or bond is a swap on an index. The credit default index (CDX) is popular in the United States, as is iTraxx in Europe, and these function in the same way in terms of payout on default or credit events.

> **Learning objective: Describe how securitized and structured products were used by investor groups and describe the consequences of their increased use.**

All banks have to pay for the assets held on their balance sheet. The same applies for individual traders. You are using repo or existing bank capital to finance the inventory you hold overnight to run your desk. Specialized yield drove investor demand, and the incentive to remove the assets from the bank's balance sheet in special-purpose vehicles was a marriage made in heaven.

Securitization and credit enhancement was able to take a BBB-rated group of securities and turn it into a AAA-rated instrument because of who got paid first and last—this is called the waterfall.

Now, under Basel I regulations, banks at the time had to hold 8% of the loans they have made on their balance sheets as opposed to turning around and selling the loan to someone else. Anything that is on the balance sheet has to have capital held against that asset in order to prevent that bank from going bankrupt. However, the regulations also said that noncontractual liquidity backstops offered to structure products had no credit charge. I guess the logic at the time was that if the liquidity promise was noncontractual, the bank could not be forced to honor it. In any event, these structured products began to move these assets off balance sheet and provide them backstop loans; and, thus, suddenly the bank had freed up additional capital for additional risk-taking activity.

Although regulatory arbitrage on the balance sheet was a big part of the problem, there was also a huge model problem as well. The easiest way to explain the problem is that the models were based on historically low default and delinquency rates. Also, there had never been a nationwide decline in housing prices since World War II, and the models simply didn't consider that kind of decline an option.

> **Learning objective: Describe how the financial crisis triggered a series of worldwide financial and economic consequences.**

There are a lot of steps here, so consider each domino but not entirely in chronological order. The ultimate trigger for the liquidity crisis was an increase in subprime mortgage defaults early in 2007. The asset-backed securities index (ABX) was an index on credit default swaps and as the value of this index falls, the cost to insure against default gets more expensive.

The equity option analogue to this would be noticing that implied volatility on equity options are higher and option prices are more expensive to use as insurance. This should cause concern about the underlying asset, which, in the case of the ABX, it did.

By May 2007, the rating agencies began to put tranches on downgrade review, which further depressed prices of these mortgage-backed products.

By mid-June 2007, large hedge funds were having problems meeting the margin calls on their credit books, forcing some fire-selling pushes to fall even lower.

© 2017 Wiley

On July 24, the National Association of Homebuilders announced that new home sales had dropped over 6%, sparking a trend that would last well into late 2008.

Although hedge funds that were invested in complex structures had some idea of how and why valuations were changing, the real earthquake was in the short-term, asset-backed commercial paper market, which is often used as a tool to borrow cash short term and fund longer-term assets. Banks began having trouble "rolling over" or redeeming their short-term paper coming due and selling new commercial paper in its place.

Companies are more likely to use the commercial paper market to fund their operations, but investment banks use repo—that is, securities lending or borrowing. This repo transaction involves collateral and is almost always considered risk free and will trade lower than Fed Funds rates. In the LIBOR (London Interbank Offered Rate) market, banks make short unsecured loans to each other. These short-term, highly secure loans are the lifeblood of the modern financial economy. The way that repo, Fed Funds, and Libor trade are relative to each other—that is, their spreads—is a key early indicator of any liquidity problems within the system.

In August 2007, many statistical quant hedge funds suffered large losses, forcing even more sales into an already declining market. By August 9, with so many funds losing so much cash, the perceived likelihood of banks' first failure began to rise as banks refused to lend to each other, driving LIBOR higher. The European central bank and the Federal Reserve both responded with liquidity injections to ease funding tensions.

Through the fall of 2007, banks had taken large write-downs on their mortgage assets, many large institutional investors such as pension funds and sovereign wealth funds "bought the bottom" in equities, and the markets sort of stabilized. However, it soon became clear, with additional stress testing, the losses taken on the write-downs were not going to be enough, and spreads widened again as the market anticipated further write-down in bank assets and lower bank stock prices.

In December 2007, the Fed announced the creation of TAF (Term Auction Facility), which basically allowed banks to borrow at the discount window and do it anonymously without the stigma previously associated with the need to go to the discount window.

The next earthquakes to hit the markets were troubles in the so-called monoline insurers. As the name implies, these companies insure single products and, in this case, it was insuring municipal bonds against default but that is as boring as it sounds. These monolines expanded into mortgage-backed securities and other securitized products, often applying the same default models to these very different products.

As losses on the mortgages mounted, the insurers themselves were on the verge of downgrade, which meant the trillions of dollars insured by these AAA monoline insurers would also fall. By January, the Fed made an emergency rate cut, the first since 1982.

The next dominoes to fall are well known, so I'll be briefer. In March 2008, Carlyle Capital was a large holder of agency bonds and, as spreads widened, took huge losses. Bear Stearns was a large creditor of Carlyle Capital. As spreads widened further and customers pulled business from Bear (along with a few misinterpreted stories in the press), Bear had trouble securing overnight repo to fund its balance sheet. Ultimately JP Morgan acquired Bear for $2 per share.

The pain didn't stop there because as delinquency rates continued to increase, spreads on Fannie Mae and Freddie Mac continued to widen. Now, these institutions are so-called government-sponsored enterprises. They have the implicit backing of the US government. In the summer of 2008, the government made that implicit guarantee explicit, but it was not enough to stop the stock price slide of Fannie and Freddie. In the fall of 2008, the government put them into conservatorship—effectively triggering a credit event—which forced huge payouts on credit default swaps.

Lehman survived a bit longer than Bear by trying to issue new equity but was unable to do so. Korea Development Bank considered a purchase, but that deal did not happen. Lehman declared bankruptcy mid-September and Merrill Lynch sold itself to Bank of America.

AIG, one of the largest of the monoline insurers of credit derivatives, announced their own liquidity problems and the Federal Reserve bought 80% of the company for $85 billion.

Because of the interconnectedness of the modern financial system, each unpredicted and nonlinear event impacts other segments of the market. Finally, to stop the ripple effects, the US Treasury set aside $80 billion to guarantee money market funds; consequently, the price of credit default swaps rose as each bank tried to protect itself against the remaining banks' credit risks.

Learning objective: Distinguish between funding liquidity and market liquidity and explain how the evaporation of liquidity can lead to a financial crisis.

Funding liquidity is the cash that professional investors (investment banks, hedge funds) use to finance the assets they are trading. Almost all these institutions use leverage, so some of their equity covers the purchase price and the balance is the typically short-term funding they have raised in the marketplace either through repo or through direct borrowing from a bank.

Market liquidity occurs when it is difficult to sell an asset without potentially influencing the price of that asset lower. You can see market liquidity dry up as bid-ask spreads widen, or if few market participants are trading in that asset or in market "resilience." That is, if a large trade moves the price of a stock lower because of low liquidity, does it stay low for an extended period of time? These are examples of limited market liquidity.

Learning objective: Analyze how an increase in counterparty credit risk can generate additional funding needs and possible systemic risk.

Think of this as a "death spiral" where stocks move lower, more people sell stocks to meet margin calls, the risk of default rises because equity moves lower, and counterparty credit risk increases. This is basically what happened in the Great Depression.

However, for the exam this is referred to as a "loss spiral"; as levered investors equity falls, they can borrow less and are forced to sell at lowered prices, pushing prices even lower. The other thing that may not be obvious about this spiral is that as asset prices move lower, the haircuts that are charged in the repo market increase and put additional pressure on collateral demands.

© 2017 Wiley

When asset prices are forced lower because of a lack of liquidity, it would seem the market would know this is temporary and actually provide more liquidity to buy the equity assets that are "on sale."

The first reason this does not happen and the loss spiral gets worse is because the absence of liquidity in the marketplace is often an indicator of increased future volatility. When uncertainty increases, margins and haircuts increase, collateral is "worth" less in repo, and the loss spiral intensifies.

The second reason is the asymmetry of information. If liquidity is low, and uncertainty is greater, then all asset buyers (of structured credit assets especially) assume the seller knows more information about that asset tranche and is selling the worst of the assets.

Gary Gorton and Andrew Metrick, 2012. "Getting Up to Speed on the Financial Crisis: A One-Weekend-Reader's Guide," *Journal of Economic Literature* 50:1, 128–150

After completing this reading, you should be able to:

- Distinguish between triggers and vulnerabilities that led to the financial crisis and their contributions to the crisis.
- Describe the main vulnerabilities of short-term debt, especially repo agreements and commercial paper.
- Assess the consequences of the Lehman failure on the global financial markets.
- Describe the historical background leading to the recent financial crisis.
- Distinguish between the two main panic periods of the financial crisis and describe the state of the markets during each.
- Assess the governmental policy responses to the financial crisis and review their short-term impact.
- Describe the global effects of the financial crisis on firms and the real economy.

This reading is almost identical to the reading Brunnermeier, *Journal of Economic Perspectives*. I'll be briefer here where there is significant overlap but you aren't missing any key concepts.

Learning objective: Distinguish between triggers and vulnerabilities that led to the financial crisis and their contributions to the crisis.

The primary trigger for the financial crisis was losses related to the subprime crisis as well as the prospect for further losses, but these triggers, in and of themselves, cannot explain the origins of the crisis.

One vulnerability was the emergence of so-called shadow banks, which are institutions outside the FDIC-regulated depository institutions that came to play a major role in either lending or designing products that were far outside the reach of regulation and oversight.

Learning objective: Describe the main vulnerabilities of short-term debt, especially repo agreements and commercial paper.

In terms of vulnerabilities, the main culprit was short-term debt such as repos and commercial paper. These markets grew exponentially leading up to the crisis. These repo markets were the key funding mechanism of the markets, but they were largely unregulated because they typically are so short term—overnight or three months—and are backed by high-quality collateral.

This begs the question: If this market is so secure, how was it a main vulnerability? As banks became less sure, counterparties could meet their repo obligations, and they either refused new repo transactions or increased the haircut on collateral, effectively "cheapening" the value of that asset to the lender. Therefore, the borrower, possibly in an already cash-strapped position, had to turn over even more collateral to fund the same balance sheet. If that wasn't possible, a forced sale was the only choice, creating a cycle of losses.

Learning objective: Assess the consequences of the Lehman failure on the global financial markets.

Money market funds are almost sacrosanct that they will always trade at $1.00. That means the NAV of the assets will be fixed at $1.00 and the assets are in the fund to support that NAV. The way money markets would maintain this is to accept cash and invest in very secure, very short-term treasury or commercial paper and earn a slice of yield. The bank would also guarantee the $1.00 NAV so the concept of "breaking the buck" where a money market fund—the shortest duration, lowest-risk product available—had to mark down assets below the dollar mark sent shockwaves through the system.

The failure of Lehman sparked this run on cash (money markets) where investors were demanding cash and the fund didn't have the assets to pay since they (commercial paper, short-term asset-backed paper) had to be marked down. The US Treasury stepped in and guaranteed money market mutual funds as a backstop, but the damage was done: Banks were hoarding liquidity at all cost, not rolling over repo, and not lending to typically secure counterparties.

Learning objective: Describe the historical background leading to the recent financial crisis.

It is interesting to note that all of the background I list here came from documents that were printed *prior* to the crisis. Most were quite telling about some of the dominos doomed to fall.

Busts often start with booms, and this boom started with the increase in issuance of asset-backed securities. Traditional banking and lending was increasingly less profitable in a low-rate environment and led to the pursuit of profits through "shadow banking" or lending activities through securitization.

With securitization also came "off balance sheet" banking where non-bank entities could offer higher returns because models could show that those products were relatively safe and the riskier tranches sold to those other asset managers who wanted that risk profile.

So there was a dual demand: holdings of unsecured (non-FDIC) money markets for extra yield the money market mutual funds search for any incremental yield. The supply of asset-backed securities met that need outside of the typical commercial banking system and led to the rise of the shadow banking system.

Basically everyone in the world was looking for yield and the seemingly safest tranche of a secured product can break the buck. (A single dollar in a money market mutual fund is no longer worth a single dollar because the assets backing the fund have dropped in value so much.) What that signals for the rest of the system is that there is also a lot of other risk that is mispriced.

> **Learning objective: Distinguish between the two main panic periods of the financial crisis and describe the state of the markets during each.**

There were two distinct periods of panic with a bit of calm between: August 2007 and September/October 2008. There are two products you want to focus on here for the exam: the asset-backed commercial paper market bank run that began in the summer of 2007 and the run on money market mutual funds in the fall of 2008.

Basic commercial paper has been used for decades and is an easy way for high-grade corporations to issue short-term debt quickly at relatively low rates and costs. These commercial paper deals also have guarantees from banks such that if investors don't buy the entire issue, the bank will create a credit line for the balance. It's a vanilla product.

Demand for commercial paper is so high that banks began to use this same idea but to bundle longer-term assets, such as accounts receivable or credit card debt, to finance even longer-term asset purchases. This type of commercial paper is called asset-backed commercial paper (ABCP) and can be moved off the balance sheet, allowing banks to save on the regulatory capital charges typically held against assets on the balance sheet.

When a bank has commercial paper maturing and cannot sell enough new commercial paper to finance the assets that are in the bundle, conceptually that is a "run" on the bank, because there are more people wanting their money back than are willing to lend to that institution.

By the end of 2007, 40% of commercial paper and ABCP programs were experiencing "runs" on the bank and could not finance the shortfall with new issuance. They had to rely on their sponsors to cover the shortfall that put even more liquidity strain on those sponsors. (A sponsor might be General Motors issuing commercial paper or JP Morgan issuing 90-day ABCP. The sponsor is who is offering the product.)

Next, we want to focus on the money market panic later in 2008. Keep in mind, money market funds are large investors in commercial paper and ABCP, but money market mutual funds are just that—highly regulated mutual funds that maintain their NAV price at $1 and can fulfill a cash request on demand. The difference between a money market mutual fund and a savings accounts is that there is FDIC protection on the savings account and not on the mutual fund (although there was a money market guarantee during the financial crisis once), because the mutual fund is investing in a little bit longer dated paper, usually 90 days and collecting some yield and passing a bit of that on to the money market holder.

Money market mutual funds (MMMFs) look for yield just like any other investor, and one MMMF held a large portion of Lehman's commercial paper so that, after the bankruptcy, they could no longer hold the NAV at $1 and they "broke the buck." The difference between the panic after Lehman and the panic in commercial paper was effectively contagion. Even though these money market funds had no connection to the mortgage losses that took down Lehman, the change in repo that the short-term MMMF liquidity relied on changed dramatically. Over 40 MMMFs eventually required support from their sponsors— and keep in mind this is a $1 trillion market—so the impact was not inconsequential.

© 2017 Wiley

Learning objective: Assess the governmental policy responses to the financial crisis and review their short-term impact.

The way I think GARP wants you to think about this is from a global scale, and the IMF data assembled in the readings came from 13 countries and was grouped into three periods: pre-Lehman, Global Crisis 1 (September 2008–December 31, 2008), and Global Crisis 2 (January 1, 2009–June 30, 2009).

With this metric, there were 153 separate policy actions across 13 countries and the full impact of these policy choices probably won't be known for decades.

To evaluate the efficacy of policy, the IMF looked at an economic stress index (ESI) and a financial stress index (FSI). The ESI is a composite of business and consumer confidence, credit spreads, stock prices of non-bank companies, and so forth. The FSI focused more on the banks such as bank prices, bank credit spreads, and bank credit. Think of this as Main Street versus Wall Street.

From the central bank rate cuts, the IMF found almost zero impact on ESI (real world) and a modest impact on FSI (Wall Street).

However, when considering central bank action such as liquidity injections, there were considerable positive impacts to FSI (release of Wall Street stress) but little impact to the real world.

So the bottom line is that across all three stages of crisis, liquidity support was helpful both to the real world and to Wall Street, but over the later periods of the crisis, direct capital injects were the most effective in their short-term impact.

Learning objective: Describe the global effects of the financial crisis on firms and the real economy.

This is a really broad learning objective and I think well known to anyone taking the exam. A few things to note: the loss of counterparty confidence among financial players jumped into the real-world lack of confidence among suppliers and consumers very quickly. That is something that happened faster than ever before partly because of the interconnectedness of the global economy.

The greatest real-world impact was the credit constraints that limited capital to the real world and was largely used to shore up the balance sheets of the larger financial institutions. That impact is still being debated.

One study found that credit-constrained companies reduced employment by an average of 11%, whereas relatively credit-unconstrained companies reduced employment by around 2%.

It is clear the postcredit demand and supply both fell, but there was an asymmetric impact on nonfinancial companies whose access to credit was limited by an as-still uncertain banking system.

STULZ, FISHER COLLEGE OF BUSINESS WORKING PAPER

René Stulz, "Risk Management Failures: What Are They and When Do They Happen?" Fisher College of Business Working Paper Series, October 2008

After completing this reading you should be able to:

- Explain how a large financial loss may not necessarily be evidence of a risk management failure.
- Analyze and identify instances of risk management failure.
- Explain how risk management failures can arise in the following areas: measurement of known risk exposures, identification of risk exposures, communication of risks, and monitoring of risks.
- Evaluate the role of risk metrics and analyze the shortcomings of existing risk metrics.

Learning objective: Explain how a large financial loss may not necessarily be evidence of a risk management failure.

We have defined the role of risk management in the first five readings of this FRM section. We will focus here on the concept that large financial losses are not necessarily a failure of risk management.

Let's limit the idea to financial risks. A company can choose to hedge financial risks that are a not a part of their core business, but that hedge may "go against" them and they could lose tens of millions of dollars. That isn't a failure of risk management; it is just the cost of not willing to bear the cost of the risk that was hedged. In other words, this is not a failure of risk management, but simply the outcome of risk management.

Now, there can be failures in risk management that do result in large losses and are a legitimate failure of risk management and not a failure of, for example, a bad trading strategy.

LTCM is the only risk failure discussed in this reading, and it wasn't a failure due to fraud but rather large market moves. LTCM was making large macro bets on volatility and correlation among assets which, when stressed, the historical relationships broke down. Since this failure wasn't due to fraud and the managers of the fund thought they were hedged, this is, in fact, a failure of management.

Lessons learned: Reduce exposure to companies whose only source of revenue is trading. In other words, face "real" companies to reduce counterparty risk since their performance is likely not directly correlated with financial asset performance.

1. Always include liquidity risk in the total risk of the position.
2. There should be broader adoption by the marketplace of positions. (This really didn't gain ground until the most recent crisis. Even so, centrally cleared swaps are only the tip of the iceberg.)
3. Apply stress testing in credit risk simulations. This helps to answer what happens when counterparties begin to fail simply due to the failure of other institutions. This has obvious relevance for the 2007–2010 crisis.

> **Learning objective: Explain how risk management failures can arise in the following areas: measurement of known risk exposures, identification of risk exposures, communication of risks, and monitoring of risks.**

First and foremost is the choice of the risk metric we are using to gauge exposures in the portfolio. If this first choice is wrong, then there could be failures in risk management simply because management is acting on wrong information. This subjective choice of measurement is one of the most critical. Even when the choice is made about how to measure a risk, those risks could be mismeasured or important risks could be ignored in the risk management process.

MEASUREMENT OF KNOWN RISK

This is the case where the right metrics have been chosen but the risks have been measured incorrectly. The measurement of risk focuses on the measurement, and prediction, of the range of future outcomes and the outliers. The mismeasurement could come in the error around the estimate of the frequency of losses or the magnitude of losses when they occur. This is why backtesting a VaR model to see how many exceedences the model throws versus how many exceedances there were in the real world is important. Additionally, there could be an error in the estimate of correlations among asset returns which could lead to losses larger than expected. This is especially important to understand within the credit VaR space.

IDENTIFICATION OF RISK EXPOSURES

There are two types you need to know for the exam: the ignored but known risks and the unknown risks. In many institutions, there are portfolios or assets that are managed separately from the core business. These are often referred to as "legacy assets" or "bad bank" assets that aren't a part of the core business. We aren't talking about those risks when we talk about identification of risk exposures.

At the trading desk level, there are credit risks, market risks, and even operational risks within aspects of counterparty credit risk management. The frequency of the change of risk means, on an ongoing basis, firms can also have risks that are "hidden" due to their complexity and due to their rapidly changing nature (high gamma). Risk management fails to capture the actual risks as quickly as the risk is changing. This is why GARP focuses on the timeliness of the risk-capture methodology in the enterprise risk management process. When managers assume there is some "gray" area around risk reporting but are comfortable, for whatever reason, knowing they may not have a complete risk inventory is an ignored but known risk. There are many examples of large losses due to incomplete inventory or incomplete risk assessment and this shouldn't be taken lightly.

The unknown risks are those that are of such low probability that they will not and cannot impact managerial decisions. An asteroid strike is an example of an unknown risk. We know it might happen, and if it does, we have much larger problems so we are going to remove it from risk planning. An extreme example but you get the idea.

COMMUNICATION OF RISK

The idea here is that risk management exists solely to inform decision making and if the results of a properly assessed and measured risk run aren't communicated in the right way, this in turn can also lead to risk management failures. As a matter of fact, a report

UBS published for its shareholders as an examination into the cause of the subprime write downs noted risk management had made several attempts to warn the board about the subprime exposure but noted the risks were communicated in a complex way using old data and didn't convey the severity of the risk. This is a clear example of correct risk management incorrectly communicated that came at a heavy price.

MONITORING OF RISK

The key issue here is the firm is taking the risks it wants and is hedging the risks it doesn't want to take. The other issue with respect to derivatives risk is the nonlinear nature of the risk and the high gamma some types of derivatives exhibit. This is why a very "granular" or at least daily risk measurement is made. Monitoring at the trading desk level can be in real time of course but for other assets that are more illiquid but still have the same sensitivity to market conditions, a daily mark to market is necessary if possible.

The clear example of this is AAA holders of residential mortgage-backed securities who used the value of the ABX index as a proxy of value had crushing losses in 2007 as the value of that index, for some mortgages issued in a certain year, were more than cut in half—an unheard of loss for a supposedly AAA security.

Bottom line: Risk can change very quickly in unexpected places and consistent and frequent risk monitoring is critical.

Learning objective: Evaluate the role of risk metrics and analyze the shortcomings of existing risk metrics.

What you want to focus on here for the exam are the limitations of existing risk metrics. The obvious role of risk metrics is to provide a quantitative assessment of risk. The problem arises when those assessments, such as VaR, have known limitations that are ignored or not understood by those using the tools. Understanding why assets don't behave according to a normal distribution is critical to understanding why VaR has many shortcomings with respect to the severity of risks. Knowing that risk exists, and also knowing extreme value theory, is a compliment to risk assessment under VaR is what you need to know. The reading doesn't go into anything new with respect to limitations: Historic data tells us little about a distribution, correlations change over time, volatility exists in "regimes" over large periods of time that can shift higher or lower as market conditions change and if these changes aren't incorporated into the models, we will have a mismeasurement of risk and the loop is complete.

Elton, Chapter 13

Edwin J. Elton, Martin J. Gruber, Stephen J. Brown, and William N. Goetzmann, Modern Portfolio Theory and Investment Analysis, 9th Edition (Hoboken, NJ: John Wiley & Sons, 2014). Chapter 13. The Standard Capital Asset Pricing Model

After completing this reading you should be able to:

- Understand the derivation and components of the CAPM.
- Describe the assumptions underlying the CAPM.
- Interpret the capital market line.
- Apply the CAPM in calculating the expected return on an asset.
- Interpret beta and calculate the beta of a single asset or portfolio.

Learning objective: Understand the derivation and components of the CAPM.

While it is important to know how to derive CAPM, it is really difficult to do this on a multiple choice exam. What can they ask you? Probably if you see something like this it will be in a "conversation" between someone and their manager with the answers describing different ways to derive the CAPM. Here is what you need to know:

The must-know formula: For some Portfolio X

$$E(R_f) = R_f + \frac{E(R_m) - R_f}{\sigma_m} \sigma_X$$

The "standard" definitions you need to know

The market price of risk is described as the incremental return that the market is offering for taking extra risk and is the term:

$$\frac{E(R_m) - R_f}{\sigma_m}$$

This could be described as the risk-free rate of return plus the market price of risk times the risk that is being taken in a particular portfolio.

The ratio above represents the **market price of risk**, *the return premium demanded by investors for each additional unit of risk (standard deviation of return) borne.*

It is only a logical step to show that movement up and to the right in a straight line (increased risk and increased return) or lower and to the left (lower risk and return) is driven by the risk taken in an individual portfolio (beta). Which gets us:

$$R_x = R_f + \beta_x(R_m - R_f)$$

In words: The return of portfolio X is the risk-free rate of return + the product of the beta of portfolio X times the return of the overall market minus the risk-free rate of return.

Now since beta is the risk of our portfolio divided by the variance of the market (the reason there is a difference in sign is the risk of portfolio X also includes one term for the risk of the market portfolio . . . don't get hung up on this detail).

$$\beta = \frac{\sigma_x}{\sigma_m^2}$$

it reduces to our original equation:

$$E(R_X) = R_f + \frac{E(R_m) - R_f}{\sigma_m}\sigma_X$$

and that is how we derive CAPM.

Learning objective: Describe the assumptions underlying the CAPM.

By developing the concept of the market price of risk and the inclusion of risk-free assets in portfolios, an asset pricing model called the **Capital Asset Pricing Model (CAPM)** was created. The CAPM, expressed as a formula below, makes the following assumptions:

- As with all mean-variance analysis, it is assumed that investors only need know the expected returns, the variances, and covariances of returns to determine optimal portfolios.
- Investors have homogenous expectations regarding the expected returns, the variances, and covariances of returns between assets.
- Investors can buy or sell any amount of any asset without affecting the asset's price, and all assets are marketable.
- Investors can borrow and lend at the risk-free rate; moreover, they can sell short any asset.
- There are no taxes on returns or transaction costs on trading activity.

The net effect of these assumptions, when combined with mean-variance analysis, is that:

- All investors have the same risk-free asset and tangency portfolio from which to construct optimal portfolios.
- The tangency portfolio is the market portfolio containing *all* risky assets, each represented in proportion to the ratio of its market capitalization to the market's entire capitalization.
- The capital allocation line for all investors is the same.
- The expected return of any asset or portfolio can be described by the CAPM equation, whose graph is called the **Security Market Line (SML)**:

$$E(R_i) = R_F + \beta_i(E(R_M) - R_F)$$

Where:

$E(R_p)$ = expected return of asset (of portfolio) i
R_F = risk-free rate of return
$E(R_M)$ = expected rate of return of the market portfolio
$\beta_1 = \dfrac{\text{Cov}(R_i, R_M)}{\text{Var}(R_M)}$

Learning objective: Interpret the capital market line.

The capital market line (CML), when graphed so that standard deviation is along the x-axis and return is on the y-axis, runs from the y-intercept (which is the risk-free rate of return) to the market portfolio at the point of tangency to the efficient frontier. Thus, the CML inherently assumes that investors will hold some linear combination of the risk-free asset and the market portfolio. In the U.S., such a combination can be emulated by holding a combination of T-bills and a broad equity index fund.

The equation of the CML adds the risk-free rate and becomes:

Equation of CML:

$$E(R_p) = R_f \sigma + \dfrac{E(R_m) - R_f}{\sigma_m} \times p$$

Graphically, the CML looks like this:

Figure 1: Capital Market Line

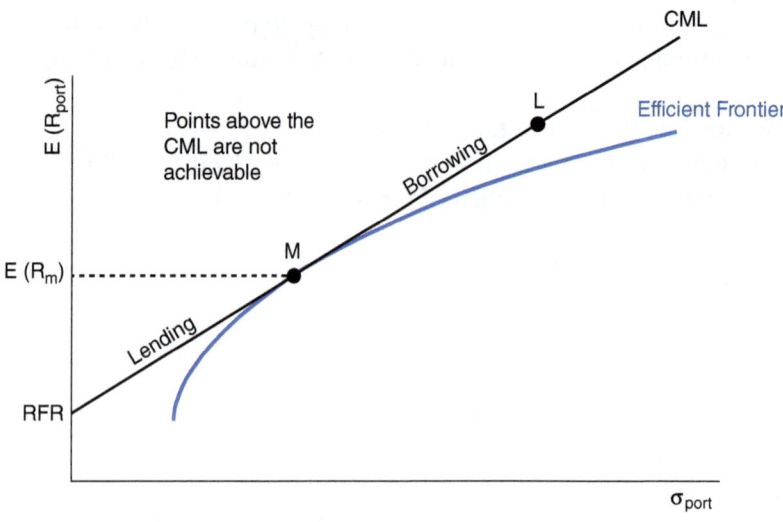

Learning objective: Apply the CAPM in calculating the expected return on an asset.

AIM statement: Interpret beta and calculate the beta of a single asset or portfolio.

Beta is a measure of the sensitivity of an asset's return to the market's return. It is computed as the covariance of the return on the asset and the return on the market divided by the variance of the market.

$$\beta_i = \frac{Cov(R_i, R_m)}{\sigma_m^2} = \frac{\rho_{i,m}\sigma_i,\sigma_m}{\sigma_m^2} = \frac{\rho_{i,m}\sigma_i}{\sigma_m}$$

Important Points Regarding Beta

1. Beta captures an asset's systematic or nondiversifiable risk.
2. A positive beta suggests that the return on the asset follows the overall trend in the market.
3. A negative beta indicates that the return on the asset generally follows a trend that is opposite to that of the current market trend.
4. A beta of zero means that the return on the asset is uncorrelated with market movements.
5. The market has a beta of 1. Therefore, the average beta of stocks in the market also equals 1.

Amenc, Chapter 4

Noel Amenc and Veronique Le Sourd, *Portfolio Theory and Performance Analysis* (West Sussex, England: John Wiley & Sons, 2003). Chapter 4. Applying the CAPM to Performance Measurement: Single-Index Performance Measurement Indicators (Section 4.2 only)

After completing this reading you should be able to:

- Calculate, compare, and evaluate the Treynor ratio, the Sharpe ratio, and Jensen's alpha.
- Compute and interpret tracking error, the information ratio, and the Sortino ratio.

Learning objective: Calculate, compare, and evaluate the Treynor ratio, the Sharpe ratio, and Jensen's alpha.

The Sharpe ratio is used to compute excess returns per unit of total risk. It is calculated as:

$$\text{Sharpe ratio} = \frac{R_p - R_f}{\sigma_p}$$

Notice that the Sharpe ratio basically equals the slope of the CAL. A portfolio with a higher Sharpe ratio is preferred to one with a lower Sharpe ratio given that the numerator of the portfolios being compared is positive. If the numerator is negative, the ratio will be closer to zero (less negative) for riskier portfolios, resulting in distorted rankings. Two drawbacks of the Sharpe ratio are that it uses total risk as a measure of risk even though only systematic risk is priced, and that the ratio itself is not informative.

The Treynor ratio basically replaces total risk in the Sharpe ratio with systematic risk (beta). It is calculated as:

$$\text{Treynor ratio} = \frac{R_p - R_f}{\beta_p}$$

Jensen's alpha is based on systematic risk (like the Treynor ratio). It first estimates a portfolio's beta risk using the market model, and then uses the CAPM to determine the required return from the investment (given its beta risk). The difference between the portfolio's actual return and the required return (as predicted by the CAPM) is called Jensen's alpha. Jensen's alpha is calculated as:

$$\alpha_p = R_p - [R_f + \beta_p(R_m - R_f)]$$

Jensen's alpha for the market equals zero. The higher the Jensen's alpha for a portfolio, the better its risk-adjusted performance.

And now for a quick summary of return, Sharpe, Treynor, and Jensen's alpha.

The following table provides information about the portfolio performance of three investment managers:

Manager	Return	σ	β
A	13%	20%	0.6
B	11%	15%	1.1
C	12%	10%	0.8
Market (M)	10%	16%	
Risk-free rate (R_f)	4%		

1. Calculate the following for each of the investment managers:
   a. Expected return
   b. Sharpe ratio
   c. Treynor ratio
   d. Jensen's alpha

> **Solution**
> 1. We illustrate the calculations for Manager A. The table that follows summarizes the results for all managers.
>
>   **Manager A**
>
>   Expected return = $R_f + \beta(R_m - R_f) = 4\% + [0.6 \times (10\% - 4\%)] = 7.6\%$
>
>   Sharpe ratio = $\dfrac{R_A - R_f}{\sigma_A} = \dfrac{13\% - 4\%}{20\%} = 0.45$
>
>   Treynor ratio = $\dfrac{R_A - R_f}{\beta_A} = \dfrac{13\% - 4\%}{0.6\%} = 0.15$
>
>   Jensen's alpha = $R_A - [R_f + \beta(R_m - R_f)] = 13\% - [4\% + 0.6(10\% - 4\%)] = 5.4\%$

Learning objective: Compute and interpret tracking error, the information ratio, and the Sortino ratio.

I don't think you will get a "Compute" question on tracking errors, but you could see a calculation problem related to the information ratio and Sortino ratios.

> *TrackingError = σ(ActiveReturn − BenchmarkReturn)*

Tracking error is an important concept and will become increasingly important in later content. The tracking error is important because it describes the deviation of our own portfolio from a benchmark portfolio. Consequently, this is used in the analysis of funds that track the benchmark. In many cases, fund managers have the ability to deviate from the composition of the benchmark to use their judgment to invest either in greater amounts of a certain security or hold more cash than the underlying benchmark. In this sense, tracking error finds the net contribution of a portfolio manager to a portfolio's returns. Therefore, it should not be assumed that tracking error is always a bad thing; it's simply a representation of the deviation from the underlying benchmark. In short, the lower the value of the tracking error, the closer we are to benchmark.

It should be noted that the additional return earned by taking either more risk or less risk than the benchmark is defined as alpha. However, it is not sufficient only to look at the increase in return we've obtained from deviating from the index. We must also consider the extra return earned within the context of the additional risk taken to earn that extra return. This idea leads us to the information ratio. The information ratio attempts to break down the excess return earned by a portfolio manager over a benchmark relative to the incremental risk taken to earn that excess return. In the information ratio, the tracking error formula makes up the denominator. The numerator is the expected return of our portfolio minus the expected return of our benchmark. The idea with the information ratio is to make sure that the incremental risk that the manager takes within the portfolio outside of the benchmark is rewarded with incremental return. This idea is consistent within other measures of portfolio management such that excess risk should be compensated in the form of excess return.

The **information ratio** is a concept similar to the Sharpe ratio:

$$IR = \frac{\bar{R}_P - \bar{R}_B}{s(R_P - R_B)}$$

The numerator is the difference between the sample mean return of the portfolio and the sample mean return of the benchmark. Dividing by the tracking risk, it expresses an excess return per unit of risk, like the Sharpe ratio. It is a measure of the extent to which an investment manager is beating a benchmark, relative to how much excess volatility the manager takes on to achieve that level of performance. This ratio could also be characterized as the residual return of an active portfolio compared to its residual risk.

The Sortino ratio is defined according to the same principle as the Sharpe ratio; however, the risk-free rate in this case is replaced with what is called the minimal acceptable return. For example, an institutional investor may define his or her return requirements as being 200 basis points above the risk-free rate of return. That return then can be plugged into the minimum accepted required return. The formula for the Sortino ratio is listed below.

$$S = \frac{R - T}{DR}$$

where R is the realized return, T is the minimum accepted return, and DR is the downside risk.

Bodie, Chapter 10

Zvi Bodie, Alex Kane, and Alan J. Marcus, *Investments*, 10th Edition (New York: McGraw-Hill, 2013). Chapter 10, Arbitrage Pricing Theory and Multifactor Models of Risk and Return

After completing this reading you should be able to:

- Describe the inputs, including factor betas, to a multifactor model.
- Calculate the expected return of an asset using a single-factor and a multifactor model.
- Describe properties of well-diversified portfolios and explain the impact of diversification on the residual risk of a portfolio.
- Explain how to construct a portfolio to hedge exposure to multiple factors.
- Describe and apply the Fama-French three factor model in estimating asset returns.

Learning objective: Describe the inputs, including factor betas, to a multifactor model.

APT seeks to describe return in ways beyond the strict assumptions about means and variances that CAPM tries to impose on its model of returns.

APT also introduces the idea of a "process." Looking ahead to the quantitative section, a process is a mathematical term that describes the behavior of a random variable (e.g., the return of an asset).

So we look to APT to explicitly model the factors that underlie behavior of individual assets then say that these prices must be arbitrage free.

We then establish elements that our portfolio has sensitivity to ... for example, we say our portfolio is sensitive to global bond returns, inversely correlated with currencies, and directly related to rainfall in Brazil. The inclusion of the last element in the list is intentional because we can subjectively choose the elements our portfolio is sensitive to under APT.

Stated formulaically:

$$E(R_p) = R_F + \lambda_1 \beta_{p,1} + \ldots \lambda_k \beta_{p,K}$$

Where:

- $E(R_F)$ = expected return on portfolio p
- R_F = risk-free rate
- $\beta_{p,i}$ = sensitivity of the portfolio return to the ith factor
- λ_i = **factor risk premium (or factor price)**, *represents the expected return, in excess of the risk-free rate, for a portfolio with a sensitivity of 1 to factor i and 0 to all other factors.* Such a portfolio configuration represents a **pure factor portfolio** for factor i.

Note how similar this equation is to the multifactor model. The return is expressed as a linear combination of the factor sensitivities and the risk premium for each factor. In this case, the portfolio is assumed to be well diversified, which is not necessarily the case for a multifactor model (recall, we showed examples for one- and two-stock portfolios).

Recall that the intercept of the multifactor model equation was considered the investment's expected return in the absence of any surprises or unexpected changes in factor values. The APT equation provides an expected return for a portfolio or asset, given equilibrium conditions. So if equilibrium holds, the APT can provide a value for the intercept of a multifactor model.

Learning objective: Calculate the expected return of an asset using a single-factor and a multifactor model.

Think back to the CAPM model and the idea of beta. In a single-factor model we have a single indicator of market performance, beta, in which we relate expected return to overall market performance. With a multifactor model, we are extending this idea to base the expected return of a company on multiple factors.

A multifactor model could be as simple as relating the expected return of a stock to GDP in its home country and the price of oil. How we arrive at these factors and what weights we give them, we will discuss later.

Mathematically our multifactor model would look like this:

$$E(R_i) = \beta_{iOil} Oil + \beta_{iGDP} GDP + \varepsilon_i$$

Never forget the error term in APT analysis. This is the explicit acknowledgment that the two factors, or however many factors you are using, are incapable of completely capturing all sources of variation in the expected return of the stock.

The Law of One Price says that for assets that have identical cash flows and identical risk profiles all should trade for the same price regardless of what they actually are. If we can show a Brazilian tree farm and a U.S. Treasury bond have the exact same cash and risk characteristics, they should trade for the same price.

You will see this concept again when we talk about creating a replicating portfolio which is the basis of all derivatives pricing and whose core idea is rooted in creating identical cash flows from two different products so we can justify the price of one asset based on the other asset—hence, a derivative.

Learning objective: Describe properties of well-diversified portfolios and explain the impact of diversification on the residual risk of a portfolio.

This is the cornerstone of modern portfolio theory and is covered in more detail in other readings. Note that the key to effectively diversifying a portfolio is to include assets whose expected returns are not perfectly correlated with each other. **Imperfect (or even negative) correlation** *allows for reductions in risk without as much reduction in expected return.*

Learning objective: Explain how to construct a portfolio to hedge exposure to multiple factors.

This section is a bit math heavy, but note that the AIM statement says to *explain*, not *calculate*, which is much more straightforward.

Recall from our single-factor model that we have a sensitivity to the beta factor of one particular security. For a portfolio of single-factor models (stocks whose return we are modeling as single factors), we have weighted betas to reflect that proportion of the security to the total portfolio.

Now with a multifactor model, we move beyond beta as the driver of returns and create a model of returns based on multiple factors such as GDP, interest rates, price of oil, etc.

Once we have a multifactor model for our portfolio of securities, we can use the factor weights to hedge any or all of our exposure to multiple factors.

Return to the oil and GDP model:

$$E(R_i) = \beta_{iOil} Oil + \beta_{iGDP} GDP + \varepsilon_i$$

Let's assume we have modeled returns with these factors:

$$E(R_i) = 1.5_{iOil} Oil + .25_{iGDP} GDP + \varepsilon_i$$

If oil goes up by 5% we expect to earn 7.5% + 25 basis points of GDP. To construct a portfolio to hedge these factors, all we have to do is take the opposite position. Simply put, instead of hedging beta in a single-factor model, we hedge the individual factors in the multifactor model.

Learning objective: Describe and apply the Fama-French three factor model in estimating asset returns.

THE CAPITAL ASSET PRICING MODEL (CAPM)
The major insight of the Capital Asset Pricing Model (CAPM) is that only systematic (non-diversifiable) risk is priced. The expected return on an asset is calculated as:

Required return on i = Expected risk-free rate + Beta$_i$ (Equity risk premium)

- Beta measures the sensitivity of an asset's returns to the returns of the market portfolio (typically a broad value-weighted equity market index).
- Beta is calculated as the covariance of the asset's returns with the returns on the market portfolio divided by the variance of returns of the market portfolio.

> **Example 1: Calculating the Required Return on Equity**
>
> Given a beta of 1.15, an equity risk premium of 7%, and a risk-free rate of 4.5%, calculate the required rate of return on the stock.
>
> **Solution**
>
> Required return = 4.5% + 1.15 (7%) = 12.55%

MULTIFACTOR MODELS

Multifactor models consider multiple (more than one) factors when estimating the required return (as opposed to the CAPM which is a single-factor model). For example, Arbitrage Price Theory (APT) models estimate required return based on a set of risk premia:

Required return = Risk-free rate + (Risk premium)$_1$ + (Risk premium)$_2$ + . . . + (Risk premium)$_k$

Risk premium$_i$ = Factor sensitivity$_i$ × Factor risk premium$_i$

- Factor sensitivity (or factor beta) refers to the asset's sensitivity to a particular factor, holding all other factors constant.
- The factor risk premium for factor i is the expected excess return (above the risk-free rate) that accrues on an asset that has a sensitivity equal to 1 to factor i and zero sensitivity to all other factors.
- The RMRF parameter is the market return minus the risk-free rate.

Other multifactor models are discussed below:

> The Fama-French model (FF model) attempts to account for the higher (than predicted by the CAPM) return on small cap stocks. This model estimates the required return as:

$$r_i = R_F + \beta_t^{mkt} RMRF + \beta_t^{size} SMB + \beta_t^{value} HML$$

β_{mkt} = Market beta
β_{size} = Size beta
β_{value} = Size beta

The FF model considers the following factors:

1. Equity risk premium (RMRF). The FF model shares this factor with the CAPM. The equity risk premium is calculated as the difference between the return on a value-weighted market index and the risk-free rate.
    - The baseline value for the market beta is 1.
    - RMRF = $R_M - R_F$.
2. Small-cap return premium (SMB). This factor accounts for differences in company market capitalizations. It is estimated as the difference between the average return on three small-cap portfolios and the average return on three large-cap portfolios.
    - The baseline value for the size beta is zero.
    - It is usually positive (negative) for small-cap (large-cap) stocks.

- SMB (small minus big) = $R_{small} - R_{big}$.
- The smaller the company, the greater the required return.

3. Value return premium (HML). This factor accounts for differences in returns on value stocks and growth stocks. It is estimated as the difference between the average return on two high book-to-market (HBM) portfolios (that represent a value bias) and the average return on two low book-to-market (LBM) portfolios (that represent a growth bias).

- The baseline value for the value beta is zero.
- It is usually positive (negative) for stocks with high (low) book-to-market ratios.
- HML (high minus low) = $R_{HBM} - R_{LBM}$.
- The higher the ratio of book-to-market, the greater the required return.

Following is an example to illustrate the difference between the two:

> **Example 2: Calculating the Required Return on Equity Based on the CAPM and FMM**
>
> An analyst gathered the following estimates regarding Violet Inc's stock:
>
> | | CAPM | FFM |
> | --- | --- | --- |
> | Current risk-free interest rate | 4.0% | 4.0% |
> | Equity market return | 9.6% | 9.6% |
> | Market beta | 1.02 | 1.11 |
> | Size beta | | –0.25 |
> | Historical size premium | | 2.8% |
> | Value beta | | –0.35 |
> | Historical value premium | | 4.4% |
>
> Calculate the required return on Violet's stock based on the CAPM and FFM. Also comment on whether the company's cost of equity benefits from its above-average market capitalization.
>
> **Solution**
>
> **CAPM**
>
> Required return = 0.04 + [1.02 (0.096 – 0.04)] = 9.71%
>
> **FFM**
>
> Required return = 0.04 + [1.11 (0.096 – 0.04)] + [(–0.25) × 0.028] + [(–0.35) × 0.044] = 7.98%
>
> Since the size premium is positive and the company has negative exposure to it, the company's above-average market capitalization serves to reduce its required return on equity.
>
> Note that the FFM market beta is usually different from the CAPM market beta because the FFM accounts for factors other than just the market factor.

BASEL COMMITTEE ON BANKING SUPERVISION

"Principles for Effective Data Aggregation and Risk Reporting" (Basel Committee on Banking Supervision Publication, January 2013)

After completing this reading you should be able to:

- Explain the potential benefits of effective risk data aggregation and reporting.
- Describe key governance principles related to risk data aggregation and risk-reporting practices.
- Identify the data architecture and IT infrastructure features that can contribute to effective risk data aggregation and risk-reporting practices.
- Describe characteristics of a strong risk data aggregation capability and demonstrate how these characteristics interact with one another.
- Describe characteristics of effective risk-reporting practices.

Learning objective: Explain the potential benefits of having effective risk data aggregation and reporting.

This reading deals with *risk data*, not the risk of data loss. This is a hugely important distinction because during the worst of the credit crisis, it became clear that the risk data, how much risk is being taken, what subsidiary is it in, and under what conditions the risk calculations were created, were all inconsistently produced and inconsistently available to senior management when they were most needed.

Obviously a situation like this creates problems for decision making, crisis management, and accurate hedging or profits and losses on any given day, especially in illiquid credit instruments.

The potential benefit of risk data aggregation is the resolution of all of these. Very ambitious but the issue of consistent risk data aggregation, especailly in a crisis, becomes extremely valuable at the trading desk level and at the enterprise level.

Learning objective: Describe key governance principles related to risk data aggregation and risk reporting practices.

Principle #1 Accuracy and Integrity

Banks should aggregate and distribute data in a way that is largely automated. A shocking number of institutions still rely on spreadsheets for their risk runs. They are quick and easy to build but largely fail to consistently report data since they are so easy to modify.

Despite the focus on automation of risk data distribution, institutions should not rely on automated decision making. There should be "breaks" in the process where human decisions have to be made with respect to results, data quality, integrity, etc.

Principle #2 Completeness

Risk data should include all sources of risk—even those sources of risk held off the balance sheet or in special-purpose vehicles.

Not all risks have to be expressed via the same metric, which is actually impossible. It is not recommended for any institution to roll all risks up into a single VaR measure. However, the risk data aggregation should be the same for all types of risks and it should be clear what method of accessing a particular risk is used. Management should also be aware of the limitations of the risk assessment method used.

In other words, data pipes aggregating risk data should be the same but no one expects any institution to look at risks in the same way across risk types.

Principle #3 Timelines

Any bank should be able to produce a firm-wide, consistent, and complete report on risks on demand.

The aggregate exposures a bank should have on-demand access to are:

1. Aggregated credit exposure to large, single borrowers
2. Counterparty credit risk exposures—this is especially important for banks with exposure to the OTC derivatives market
3. Trading exposures by segmentation, geography, duration, and sector
4. Any operational risks that could lead to systemic business disruption

Principle #4 Risk data should be on-demand but adaptable

Basically banks should have access to on-demand risk data that is flexible enough to request a new type of report that would enable quick decision making in a crisis scenario. Usually this means requesting data and risk reports with a higher degree of granularity. "Our credit exposure to oil rig manufacturers based in Canada" is an example of an adaptable risk data set.

Banks should also have adaptable enough systems that additional layers of reporting capacity could be added for changing credit exposures, new business lines, or regulations.

Learning objective: Identify the data architecture and IT infrastructure features that can contribute to effective risk data aggregation and risk reporting practices.

IT is the biggest piece of this because all of these systems rely on the IT infrastructure. So, having IT backup systems that confirm and double-check results independently is a must.

Learning objective: Describe characteristics of a strong risk data aggregation capability and demonstrate how these characteristics interact with one another.

Risk aggregation is important because many systems within large institutions don't "talk" to one another. This means getting a comprehensive and consistent measure of risk exposures during times of extreme market moves—when it is needed most—is almost impossible.

Characteristics of a strong data aggregation capability are:

1. Accurate and reliable aggregation—bank should have a single, final source for each type of risk. For example, there should be a credit-risk data czar who has access to all sources of credit risk data firm-wide.
2. Automation is helpful but there should be sufficient human interaction to apply judgement where possible. Basically don't rely on the models and computers for everything.
3. The risk team should be able to generate, virtually on demand, any firm-wide report from all sources of data. This is why central repositories of risk data are so important.

Learning objective: Describe characteristics of effective risk reporting practices.

I think this list has a low probability of appearing on the exam but what you should know about the risk reporting characteristics is that they should be:

1. Accurate
2. Comprehensive
3. Clear
4. Frequently produced
5. Widely distributed

GARP Code of Conduct*

After completing this reading you should be able to:

- Describe the responsibility of each GARP member with respect to professional integrity, ethical conduct, conflicts of interest, confidentiality of information, and adherence to generally accepted practices in risk management.
- Describe the potential consequences of violating the GARP Code of Conduct.

GARP CODE OF CONDUCT

I. Introductory Statement

The GARP Code of Conduct ("Code") sets forth principles of professional conduct for Global Association of Risk Professionals (GARP), Financial Risk Management (FRM®) and Energy Risk Professional (ERP®) certifications and other GARP certification and diploma holders and candidates, GARP's board of trustees, its regional directors, GARP committee members, and GARP's staff (hereinafter collectively referred to as "GARP members") in support of the advancement of the financial risk management profession.

These principles promote the highest levels of ethical conduct and disclosure and provide direction and support for both the individual practitioner and the risk management profession.

The pursuit of high ethical standards goes beyond following the letter of applicable rules and regulations and behaving in accordance with the intentions of those laws and regulations, to pursuing a universal ethical culture.

All individuals, firms, and associations have an ethical character. Some of the biggest risks faced by firms today involve not legal or compliance violations but rather decisions involving ethical considerations and the application of appropriate standards of conduct to business decision making.

There is no single prescriptive ethical standard that can be globally applied. We can only expect that GARP* members will continuously consider ethical issues and adjust their conduct accordingly as they engage in their daily activities.

This document makes references to professional standards and generally accepted risk management practices. Risk practitioners should understand these as concepts that reflect an evolving shared body of professional standards and practices. In considering the issues this raises, ethical behavior must weigh the circumstances and the culture of the applicable global community in which the practitioner resides.

II. Code of Conduct

The Code is comprised of the following Principles, Professional Standards, and Rules of Conduct which GARP members agree to uphold and implement.

1. **Principles**

    1.1 *Professional Integrity and Ethical Conduct.* GARP members shall act with honesty, integrity, and competence to fulfill the risk professional's responsibilities and to uphold the reputation of the risk management profession. GARP members must avoid disguised contrivances in assessments, measurements, and processes that are intended to provide business advantage at the expense of honesty and truthfulness.

---

*Reprinted with permission from GARP.

1.2 *Conflicts of Interest.* GARP members have a responsibility to promote the interests of all relevant constituencies and will not knowingly perform risk management services directly or indirectly involving an actual or potential conflict of interest unless full disclosure has been provided to all affected parties of any actual or apparent conflict of interest. Where conflicts are unavoidable, GARP members commit to their full disclosure and management.

1.3 *Confidentiality.* GARP members will take all reasonable precautionary measures to prevent intentional and unintentional disclosure of confidential information.

2. **Professional Standards**

    2.1 *Fundamental Responsibilities.*

    - GARP members must endeavor, and encourage others, to operate at the highest level of professional skill.
    - GARP members should always continue to perfect their expertise.
    - GARP members have a personal ethical responsibility and cannot outsource or delegate that responsibility to others.

    2.2 *Best Practices.*

    - GARP members will promote and adhere to applicable "best practice standards," and will ensure that risk management activities performed under his/her direct supervision or management satisfies these applicable standards.
    - GARP members recognize that risk management does not exist in a vacuum. GARP members commit to considering the wider impact of their assessments and actions on their colleagues and the wider community and environment in which they work.

    2.3 *Communication and Disclosure.*

    - GARP members issuing any communications on behalf of their firm will ensure that the communications are clear, appropriate to the circumstances and their intended audience, and satisfy applicable standards of conduct.

III. Rules of Conduct

1. **Professional Integrity and Ethical Conduct**

GARP members:

1.1 Shall act professionally, ethically, and with integrity in all dealings with employers, existing or potential clients, the public, and other practitioners in the financial services industry.

1.2 Shall exercise reasonable judgment in the provision of risk services while maintaining independence of thought and direction. GARP members must not offer, solicit, or accept any gift, benefit, compensation, or consideration that could be reasonably expected to compromise their own or another's independence and objectivity.

1.3 Must take reasonable precautions to ensure that the member's services are not used for improper, fraudulent, or illegal purposes.

1.4 Shall not knowingly misrepresent details relating to analysis, recommendations, actions, or other professional activities.

1.5 Shall not engage in any professional conduct involving dishonesty or deception or engage in any act that reflects negatively on their integrity, character, trustworthiness, or professional ability or on the risk management profession.

1.6 Shall not engage in any conduct or commit any act that compromises the integrity of GARP, the (Financial Risk Manager) FRM designation, or the integrity or validity of the examinations leading to the award of the right to use the FRM designation or any other credentials that may be offered by GARP.

1.7 Shall endeavor to be mindful of cultural differences regarding ethical behavior and customs, and to avoid any actions that are, or may have the appearance of being unethical according to local customs. If there appears to be a conflict or overlap of standards, the GARP member should always seek to apply the higher standard.

2. **Conflict of Interest**

GARP members:

2.1 Shall act fairly in all situations and must fully disclose any actual or potential conflict to all affected parties.

2.2 Shall make full and fair disclosure of all matters that could reasonably be expected to impair their independence and objectivity or interfere with their respective duties to their employer, clients, and prospective clients.

3. **Confidentiality**

GARP members:

3.1 Shall not make use of confidential information for inappropriate purposes and unless having received prior consent shall maintain the confidentiality of their work, their employer, or client.

3.2 Must not use confidential information to benefit personally.

4. **Fundamental Responsibilities**

GARP members:

4.1 Shall comply with all applicable laws, rules, and regulations (including this Code) governing the GARP Members' professional activities and shall not knowingly participate or assist in any violation of such laws, rules, or regulations.

4.2 Shall have ethical responsibilities and cannot outsource or delegate those responsibilities to others.

4.3 Shall understand the needs and complexity of their employer or client, and should provide appropriate and suitable risk management services and advice.

4.4 Shall be diligent about not overstating the accuracy or certainty of results or conclusions.

4.5 Shall clearly disclose the relevant limits of their specific knowledge and expertise concerning risk assessment, industry practices, and applicable laws and regulations.

5. **Generally Accepted Practices**

GARP members:

5.1 Shall execute all services with diligence and perform all work in a manner that is independent from interested parties. GARP members should collect, analyze, and distribute risk information with the highest level of professional objectivity.

5.2 Shall be familiar with current generally accepted risk management practices and shall clearly indicate any departure from their use.

5.3 Shall ensure that communications include factual data and do not contain false information.

5.4 Shall make a distinction between fact and opinion in the presentation of analysis and recommendations.

IV. Applicability and Enforcement

Every GARP member should know and abide by this Code.

Local laws and regulations may also impose obligations on GARP members. Where local requirements conflict with the Code, such requirements will have precedence.

Violation(s) of this Code by members may result in, among other things, the temporary suspension or permanent removal of the GARP member from GARP's membership roles, and may also include temporarily or permanently removing from the violator the right to use or refer to having earned the FRM designation or any other GARP-granted designation, following a formal determination that such a violation has occurred.

Learning objective: Describe the responsibility of each GARP member with respect to professional integrity, ethical conduct, conflicts of interest, confidentiality of information, and adherence to generally accepted practices in risk management.

Professional integrity—Act responsibly, exercise reasonable judgment in the provision of risk services.

Ethical conduct—Act with honesty and integrity at all times.

Conflicts of interest—GARP members should not perform risk management services involving actual or potential conflicts of interest.

Confidentiality of information—Take all reasonable measures to avoid confidential information.

Adherence to generally accepted practices in risk management—Not surprisingly, GARP says to be familiar with best practices and apply them.

Learning objective: Describe the potential consequences of violating the GARP Code of Conduct.

The thing to know for the exam is that local law takes precedent over the Code and GARP can choose to temporarily or permanently bar an FRM designation holder from using the designation following a formal determination by GARP that a violation has occurred.

QUANTITATIVE ANALYSIS (QA)

This area tests your knowledge of basic probability and statistics. The broad areas of knowledge covered in readings related to quantitative analysis include the following:

- Discrete and continuous probability distributions
- Estimating the parameters of distributions
- Population and sample statistics
- Bayesian analysis
- Statistical inference and hypothesis testing
- Correlations and copulas
- Estimating correlation and volatility using EWMA and GARCH models
- Volatility term structures
- Linear regression with single and multiple regressors
- Time series analysis
- Simulation methods

Miller, Chapter 2

Michael Miller, *Mathematics and Statistics for Financial Risk Management*, 2nd Edition (Hoboken, NJ: John Wiley & Sons, 2013). Chapter 2. Probabilities

After completing this reading you should be able to:

- Describe and distinguish between continuous and discrete random variables.
- Define and distinguish between the probability density function, the cumulative distribution function, and the inverse cumulative distribution function.
- Calculate the probability of an event given a discrete probability function.
- Distinguish between independent and mutually exclusive events.
- Define joint probability, describe a probability matrix, and calculate joint probabilities using probability matrices.
- Define and calculate a conditional probability, and distinguish between conditional and unconditional probabilities.

Learning objective: Describe and distinguish between continuous and discrete random variables.

I think there's a very low probability that you'll actually be explicitly asked to distinguish between a continuous time and discrete random variable; however, you must be aware of the distinction for the other topics that we are to talk about. A discrete random variable is one that "acts" in discrete time periods or events that can be discretely identified.

A great example of this is the flip of a coin. Five flips denote five events, those events can be clearly identified, and therefore this represents a discrete set of events. Interesting to note that the outcome of the experiment will be driven by the rules of behavior or the distribution that we assume this random variable, in this case a coin, "acts" under. This is what a random variable in discrete time looks like:

$$X = \begin{cases} 0, & \text{if heads,} \\ 1, & \text{if tails,} \end{cases}$$

where the probability of this event assuming a fair coin is:

$$P(x) = \begin{cases} \frac{1}{2}, & \text{if } x = 0, \\ \frac{1}{2}, & \text{if } x = 1, \\ 0, & \text{otherwise,} \end{cases}$$

At this point it is worth making a small note on notation.

In the equation above we define the random variable "big X" as the outcome of an experiment. The experiment in this case is the flipping of a fair coin one time. And we don't know that the experiment is fair until we look at the next piece of information, which is referred to as the probability mass function. When we look at the continuous random variables, this will be known as the probability density function. From the probability mass function (the rules of behavior for a discreet random variable as opposed to a probability density function, which are those rules for a continuous time random variable) above, we know it is a discrete random variable because we had two discrete states of outcome.

In this case we see that we have an equal probability, in this case one half, of getting heads or tails, denoted by the variable zero or one.

A random variable that is operating in continuous time is one in which the events or the outcome could happen at increasingly small intervals of time. Alternatively, we can think of a continuous random variable as one that has infinitely smaller scales, or is one that is not defining a specific interval of time. Think of this as your basic definition of a derivative from calculus I. When the interval time gets smaller and smaller and we still can't identify an event as happening discretely, or at only one place and time, then we say that this random variable is a continuous function.

With a discrete random variable, we think of probability in terms of outcome being less than or greater than some number. With a continuous random variable, however, we think of this in terms of density, and this is an important concept. The greater the density of something, the greater the likelihood of finding that "thing" under the experiment we are considering. We will see many examples of this later; however, the key takeaway at this point is that random variables can behave either in continuous time or in discreet time.

Learning objective: Define and distinguish between the probability density function, the cumulative distribution function, and the inverse cumulative distribution function.

For a discrete random variable, the probability of each possible outcome can be listed in the form of a probability function, p(x), which expresses the probability that "X," the random variable, takes on a specific value of "x." A probability function can also be stated as $P(X = x)$.

- p(x) or $P(X = x) = 0$ means that the random variable cannot take the particular value of x.
- p(x) or $P(X = x) > 0$ means that the specified value of x is present in the set of possible outcomes that the random variable can take.
- p(x) or $P(X = x) = 1$ means that x is the only possible outcome.

For example, if the random variable, X, is the number of days it snows this December, the probability of there being 5 days of snow, p(5), or $P(X = 5)$ is greater than zero but less than one. However, p(40) or $P(x = 40)$ equals zero because it is impossible for it to snow for 40 days in a 31-day period.

A continuous random variable is one for which the number of possible outcomes cannot be counted (there are infinite possible outcomes) and therefore, probabilities cannot be attached to specific outcomes. For example, consider the length of time it takes to get served at a particular restaurant (a random variable), which can be anywhere between 25 and 40 minutes (possible outcomes). While the probability of the waiting period being between 25 and 30 minutes can be measured, the probability of waiting for exactly 25 minutes and 15 seconds is zero because time can be measured in seconds, half seconds, even thousandths of seconds. The actual period of time taken to get served can take an infinite number of values as the unit of measurement gets smaller. Other examples of continuous random variables are:

- The amount of liquid poured into a glass that can hold 10 ounces. The random variable X can lie anywhere between, and including, zero and 10 ounces.
- The amount of liquid can be measured in ounces, half ounces, thousandths of ounces, and in even smaller units. The number of possible outcomes is therefore, infinite.
- The return on a stock for a particular year. This random variable can take any value between –100% and infinity.

For continuous random variables, the probability of a specific outcome within a range of infinite outcomes is essentially zero: p(x) or P(X = x) = 0. Therefore, we use a probability density function (pdf), which is denoted by f(x) to interpret their probability structure. A pdf can be used to determine the probability that the outcome lies within a specified range of possible values. On a graphical illustration of the pdf (Figure 1), the probability that the outcome lies between a and b equals the area under the density function between the two points.

Figure 1

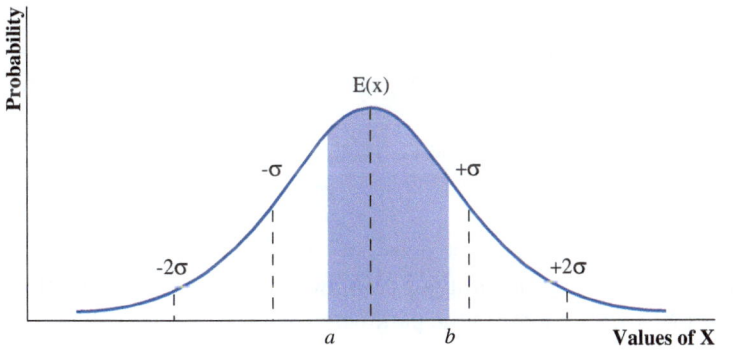

A cumulative distribution function (cdf), also known as a distribution function, expresses the probability that a random variable, X, takes on a value less than or equal to a specific value, x. It represents the sum of the probabilities of all outcomes that are less than or equal to the specified value of x. A cdf is denoted by $F(x) = P(X \leq x)$.

Learning objective: Calculate the probability of an event given a discrete probability function.

> **Example 1**
>
> The set of possible values that a random variable, X, can take is given by: X = (5,10,15,20)
> For all other values of X, p(x) = 0.
>
> The probability function for the random variable is given as: p(x) = x/50
>
> Calculate the following probabilities:
>
> a. p(5)
> b. p(15)
> c. p(17)
> d. F(10)
> e. F(20)
>
> **Solution**
>
> a. p(5) = 5/50 = 0.1
> b. p(15) = 15/50 = 0.3
> c. p(17) = 0
> d. F(10) = p(5) + p(10) = 0.1 + 0.2 = 0.3
> e. F(20) = p(5) + p(10) + p(15) + p(20) = 0.1 + 0.2 + 0.3 + 0.4 = 1.0

Learning objective: Distinguish between independent and mutually exclusive events.

DEPENDENT AND INDEPENDENT EVENTS

With two dependent events, the occurrence of one is related to the occurrence of the other.

For example, the probability of doing well on an exam is related to the probability of preparing well for it.

Two events are independent if the occurrence of one does not have any bearing on the occurrence of the other. For example, the probability of doing well on an exam is unrelated to the probability of there being exactly 5 trees in the park nearby.

When two events are independent:

$P(A|B) = P(A)$, or equivalently, $P(B|A) = P(B)$

If we are trying to forecast an event, information about a dependent event may be useful, but information about an independent event will not be useful. The results of three throws of the die are independent of each other. The probability of getting a 3 on the second throw is not related to the outcome of the first throw. The probability of rolling a 4 on each of the throws is equal.

P(getting a 4 on the first and a 4 on the second and a 4 on the third throw):
= $P(4) \times P(4) \times P(4) = (1/6) \times (1/6) \times (1/6) = 0.00463$

With independent events, the word *and* implies multiplication, and the word *or* implies addition. Therefore:

$$P(A \text{ or } B) = P(A) + P(B) - P(AB)$$
$$P(A \text{ and } B) = P(A) \times P(B)$$

Learning objective: Define joint probability, describe a probability matrix, and calculate joint probabilities using probability matrices.

Before stating an exact definition of a conditional probability, we need to define the joint probability, P(AB), which answers the question, "What is the probability of both A and B occurring?"

- If A and B are mutually exclusive events, the joint probability P(AB) equals zero. This is because mutually exclusive events cannot occur simultaneously.

    Example:
    Event A = Getting a 3 upon rolling the die.
    Event B = Getting a 4 on the same throw.
    Since a 3 and a 4 cannot be obtained on the same throw, P(AB) = 0.

- If A is contained within the set of possible outcomes for B, P(AB) = P(A).

    Example:
    Event A = Getting a 3 upon rolling the die.
    Event B = Getting an odd number upon rolling the die.
    Rolling a 3 can only occur if an odd number is rolled. Therefore, the probability of rolling a 3 and rolling an odd number, P(AB), is simply the probability of rolling a 3, P(A).

Now that we have a better understanding of joint probabilities, we can define a conditional probability, P(A|B) (the probability of event A occurring given that event B has occurred) as the joint probability, P(AB), divided by the unconditional probability of event B occurring, P(B).

PROBABILITY MATRICES

This is a probability matrix:

| | | Stock | | |
		Outperform	Underperform	
Bonds	Upgrade	35%	10%	45%
	No Change	40%	10%	50%
	Downgrade	5%	0%	5%
		80%	20%	100%

The intersection of the row and columns show the joint probability of those two events. For example, the probability of a bond upgrade and stocks outperforming is 35%. The key information here is this is the JOINT probability of both events.

Learning objective: Define and calculate a conditional probability, and distinguish between conditional and unconditional probabilities.

Conditional probabilities express the probability of an event occurring given that another event has occurred. They answer questions like "What is the probability of the return on the stock being above 10% given that the return is above the risk-free rate?" or "What is the probability of rolling a 3 given that an odd number is rolled?"

Let's differentiate between a conditional and an unconditional probability using an example. Let's calculate the unconditional probability of rolling a 3, and the conditional probability of rolling a 3 given that an odd number is rolled.

Unconditional probability of rolling a 3:

$$P(3) = 1/6 = 0.167$$

Conditional probability of rolling a 3 *given* that an odd number is rolled:

$$P(3 \mid \text{odd numbers is rolled}) = \frac{P(AB)}{P(B)} = \frac{P(\text{rolling a 3 and rolling an odd number})}{P(\text{rolling an odd number})}$$

$$= \frac{0.167}{0.5} = 0.334$$

Miller, Chapter 3

Michael Miller, *Mathematics and Statistics for Financial Risk Management*, 2nd Edition (Hoboken, NJ: John Wiley & Sons, 2013). Chapter 3. Basic Statistics

After completing this reading you should be able to:

- Interpret and apply the mean, standard deviation, and variance of a random variable.
- Calculate the mean, standard deviation, and variance of a discrete random variable.
- Interpret and calculate the expected value of a discrete random variable.
- Calculate and interpret the covariance and correlation between two random variables.
- Calculate the mean and variance of sums of variables.
- Describe the four central moments of a statistical variable or distribution: mean, variance, skewness, and kurtosis.
- Interpret the skewness and kurtosis of a statistical distribution, and interpret the concepts of coskewness and cokurtosis.
- Describe and interpret the best linear unbiased estimator.

Learning objective: Interpret and apply the mean, standard deviation, and variance of a random variable.

A measure of central tendency looks to identify the "middle" or "expected value" of a data set. The arithmetic mean is the most frequently used measure of central tendency. It is simply the sum of all the observations in a data set divided by the total number of observations. The arithmetic mean can be calculated for the entire population (μ) and for a sample (X).

For population consisting of N observations the population mean is calculated as:

$$\mu = \frac{\sum_{i=1}^{N} X_i}{N}$$

where
X_i = is the ith observations.

Properties of the Arithmetic Mean
- All observations are used in the computation of the arithmetic mean.
- All interval and ratio data sets have an arithmetic mean.
- The sum of the deviations from the arithmetic mean is always 0: $\sum_{i=1}^{n}(X_i - \bar{X}) = 0$.
- An arithmetic mean is unique (i.e., a data set only has one arithmetic mean).

A potential problem with the arithmetic mean is its sensitivity to extreme values. Because each and every observation is used in its computation, a disproportionately small or large value can drag the arithmetic mean toward itself.

For example, a data set consisting of observations of 5, 8, 7, 10, 12, and 143 has an arithmetic mean of 30.83, which is significantly larger in magnitude than the bulk of the data (the first five observations). In this case, there are doubts regarding how well the arithmetic mean represents the data.

POPULATION VARIANCE AND STANDARD DEVIATION

A more commonly used measure of dispersion is the variance, which equals the sum of the squares of deviations from the mean. The standard deviation is the positive square root of the variance. While the variance has no units, the standard deviation is expressed in the same units as the random variable itself. The variance and standard deviation can be calculated for both populations and samples.

The variance calculated using all the observations in a population is called the population variance (σ_2) and is calculated as:

$$\sigma = \sqrt{\frac{\sum_{i=1}^{N}(X_i - \mu)^2}{N}}$$

The population standard deviation (σ) is the positive square root of the population variance.

Learning objective: Calculate the mean, standard deviation, and variance of a discrete random variable.

Calculate the variance and standard deviation of the scores of five golfers assuming that they represent the entire population of golfers participating in a particular tournament.

Their scores are 67, 71, 72, 75, and 68.

$$\text{Population mean} = \mu = \frac{[67 + 71 + 72 + 75 + 68]}{5} = 70.6$$

$$\sigma^2 = \frac{[(67 - 70.6)^2 + (71 - 70.6)^2 + (72 - 70.6)^2 + (75 - 70.6)^2 + (68 - 70.6)^2]}{5} = 8.24$$

The average score of the five golfers is 70.6 strokes. The variance however, is 8.24 strokes squared. There is no such thing as strokes squared, which makes interpreting the variance very difficult. Therefore, the variance (which is always in squared units) is converted to a standard deviation, which equals the square root of the variance and is always presented in the same unit as the observations in the data set.

$$\text{Standard deviation} = \sigma = \sqrt{8.24} = 2.871 \text{ strokes.}$$

Conclusion: The average score of the five golfers is 70.6 strokes, and the standard deviation of their scores is 2.87 strokes.

Learning objective: Interpret and calculate the expected value of a discrete random variable.

Don't confuse a discrete random variable, which is one that is countable and clearly separate from other events, and the discrete uniform distribution. The expected value of any random variable is the event multiplied by its probability function. In this case, a discrete random variable will have a discrete probability function. In the simplest case, the probability function of a fair die is uniform over 1 to 6 with each probability being 1/6th and the probability of tossing a three is 1/6.

Learning objective: Calculate and interpret the covariance and correlation between two random variables.

- Covariance is a measure of the extent to which two random variables move together. For two random variables, X and Y, that have expected values of E(X) and E(Y) respectively, the covariance is calculated as:

$$Cov(XY) = E\{[X - E(X)][Y - E(Y)]\}$$

We can also write the covariance formula in terms of the returns on Asset A and Asset B:

Properties of Covariance
- Covariance is a similar concept to variance. The difference lies in the fact that variance measures how a random variable varies with itself, while covariance measures how a random variable varies with another random variable.
- Covariance is symmetric, that is, Cov(X,Y) = Cov (Y,X).
- Covariance can range from positive infinity to negative infinity. Variance, on the other hand, is always positive.
- The covariance of X with itself, Cov(X,X), is equal to variance of X, Var(X).
- When the covariance of returns of two assets is negative, it means that when the return on one asset is above its expected value, the return on the other tends to be below its expected value. There is an inverse relationship between the two variables.
- When the covariance of returns of two assets is positive, it means that when the return on one asset is above its expected value, the return on the other also tends to be above its expected value. Covariance of returns is zero if the returns are unrelated.

Limitations of Covariance
- Because the unit that covariance is expressed in depends on the unit that the data is presented in, it is difficult to compare covariance across data sets that have different scales.
- In practice, it is difficult to interpret covariance as it can take on extremely large values.

© 2017 Wiley

- Covariance does not tell us anything about the strength of the relationship between the two variables.

The formula for calculating the covariance between random variables R_A R_B is:

$$Cov(R_A, R_B) = \sum_i \sum_j P(R_{A,i}, R_{B,J})(R_{A,i} - ER_A)(R_{B,j} - ER_B)$$

Example 1: Calculating Covariance

Calculate and interpret the covariance of the returns for Stock A and Stock B given three possible states of the economy—expansion, normal, and recession. The returns of Stock A and Stock B under each state and the probability of each state are listed below.

State	P(S)	R_A	R_S
Expansion	0.25	0.04	0.02
Normal	0.36	0.08	0.01
Recession	0.39	0.01	0.04
	Σ(P) = 1.0		

Solution

First we calculate the expected return on the two stocks:

$$E(R_A) = (0.25)(0.04) + (0.36)(0.08) + (0.39)(0.01) = 0.0427$$
$$E(R_B) = (0.25)(0.02) + (0.36)(0.01) + (0.39)(0.04) = 0.0242$$

State	P(S)	R_A	R_B	$P(S)[R_A - E(R_A)][R_B - E(R_B)]$
Expansion	0.25	0.04	0.02	(0.25)(0.04 − 0.0427)(0.02 − 0.0242) = 0.00000284
Normal	0.36	0.08	0.01	(0.36)(0.08 − 0.0427)(0.01 − 0.0242) = −0.000191
Recession	0.39	0.01	0.04	(0.39)(0.01 − 0.0427)(0.04 − 0.0242) = −0.000201

The covariance of the returns of the two assets is calculated as:

$$0.00000284 + (0.000191) + (-0.000201) = -0.000389$$

The only thing that the covariance tells us is that the returns on the two assets are inversely related (indicated by the negative sign). Covariance does not tell us anything about the strength of the relationship between the two variables.

CORRELATION COEFFICIENT

The correlation coefficient measures the strength and direction of the linear relationship between two random variables. It is obtained by dividing (standardizing) the covariance of the two random variables by the product of their standard deviations.

$$Corr(R_A, R_B) = (R_A, R_B) = \frac{Cov(R_A, R_B)}{(\sigma_A)(\sigma_B)}$$

Properties of the Correlation Coefficient
- It measures the strength of the relationship between two random variables.
- It has no unit.
- It lies between −1 and +1.
- A correlation coefficient of +1 indicates a perfect positive correlation between two random variables.
- A correlation coefficient of −1 indicates a perfect negative correlation between two random variables.
- A correlation coefficient of zero indicates no linear relationship between two random variables.

A shortcoming of the correlation coefficient is the fact that it does not specify which factor or variable causes the linear relationship between the two variables.

Example 2: Correlation Coefficient

Using the data in Example 1, compute the correlation coefficient given that the variance of Stock A is 0.123 and the variance of Stock B is 0.325.

$$\sigma_A = \sqrt{0.123} = 0.351$$
$$\sigma_B = \sqrt{0.325} = 0.57$$
$$\text{Corr}(R_A, R_B) = -0.000389 / (0.351)(0.57) = -0.00195$$

The correlation between the returns on the two assets is very close to zero. We can conclude that their returns are uncorrelated.

Learning objective: Calculate the mean and variance of sums of variables.

The reason this is important right now is because an entire portfolio can be expressed as a single random variable.

$$E(R_p) = \sum_{i=1}^{N} w_i E(R_i) = w_1 E(R_1) + w_2 E(R_2) + \ldots + w_N E(R_N)$$

If we can describe multiple possible portfolios, each with their own mean and variance, we want to calculate the mean and variance of the sum of portfolios as well.

This is the basis of diversification. A single security becomes a portfolio of two securities. Then we add to that another portfolio of two securities and see how that changes the mean, variance profile.

For the exam know that means sum according to the weight within the portfolio but because of correlation, the variance of a sum of portfolios is not the sum of its variances—in other words, the sum is different from its parts.

To calculate the mean and variance of sums of variables (portfolios of securities) we use the same formulas as before for the expectation (mean) and variance.

The expected return and the variance of returns for a portfolio of assets are based on the properties of the individual assets in the portfolio. The first step in calculating portfolio expected return and variance is to compute the weights of the individual assets comprising the portfolio.

$$\text{Weight of asset } i = \frac{\text{Market value of investment } i}{\text{Market value of portfolio}}$$

The expected value of returns on a portfolio is a function of the returns on the individual assets and of their respective weights.

Calculating the variance of a portfolio is more complicated. The variance is not only a function of individual asset weights and variances, but also of the covariance of the assets with each other.

$$\text{Var}(R_p) = \sum_{i=1}^{N}\sum_{j=1}^{N} w_i w_j \text{Cov}(R_i, R_j)$$

The variance of a two-asset portfolio that contains only Asset A and Asset B is given as:

$$\text{Var}(R_p) = w_A^2 \sigma^2(R_A) + w_B^2 \sigma^2(R_B) + 2 w_A w_B \text{Cov}(R_A, R_B)$$

Learning objective: Describe the four central moments of a statistical variable or distribution: mean, variance, skewness, and kurtosis.

Note: this is extremely important across at least half of the FRM exam. You will see this in hypothesis testing, CAPM, mean-variance analysis, and so forth. Almost every element of risk management is described by these four characteristics.

Mean is the simple average of the distribution and is called the first moment. So by analogy, the first moment of a portfolio is its expected return. Understanding the statistical moments in relation to their portfolio or CAPM analog is a really important way to build intuition.

The variance is called the second moment and describes the deviation away from the expectation of a distribution.

Skewness is called the third moment and describes how asymmetric a distribution is. For portfolio management, investors care only about the expected return and risk (mean and variance) of a portfolio and whether they can ignore skewness, kurtosis, and other attributes of a distribution.

Kurtosis describes how much "mass" or how likely extreme events are to occur. A high degree of kurtosis means there is more mass in the tails, extreme events (black swans) are more likely, and in order for a distribution to have more mass in the tails, it must have a shorter "peak" than a typical normal distribution.

So guess what the mean of a stock portfolio is called? Its beta. What about a bond portfolio? It's DV01. Variance then is the expectation away from those first moment estimates, and the more "moments" we add, the more accurate our prediction. Guess what the rate of change in a first moment is called? It's the second moment. Recall from calculus that the rate of change of the average is the second derivative. This is all exactly the same concept. The rate of change of delta for an options portfolio (the expectation of that random variable) is the second derivative, a.k.a. second moment a.k.a. gamma. This is probably the single most important thing to understand about quantifying financial risk in the entire FRM program.

Learning objective: Interpret the skewness and kurtosis of a statistical distribution, and interpret the concepts of coskewness and cokurtosis.

Skewness tells us how symmetric a distribution around the mean is and is described in two ways: either positive or negative skew. Where the most mass of a distribution lies relative to its mean will tell us if a distribution is positively or negatively skewed, but visually this looks counterintuitive. A positive skew distribution looks like Figure 1.

Figure 1

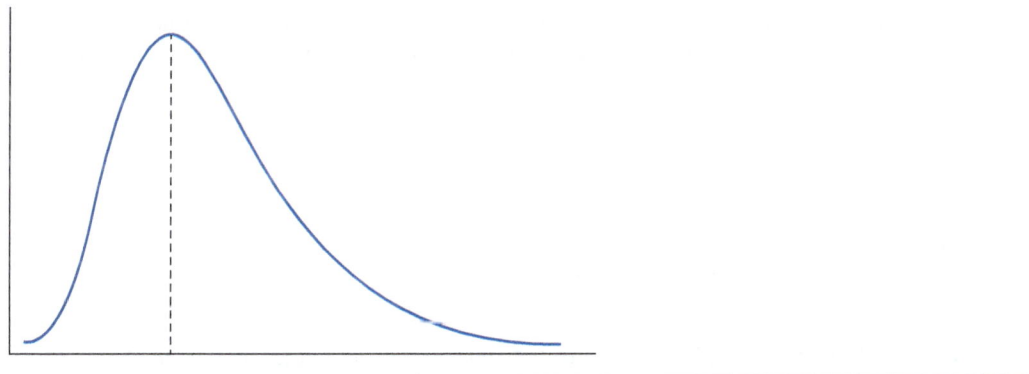

With a positive skew distribution, the peak is "skewed" toward the right or negative side. But from the perspective of where the most mass is, look at the right side and visually you can see that is where the most "mass" or events will probabilistically occur. Therefore this is called a positive or right skewed distribution, and vice versa.

Remember how the kurtosis of a distribution is the third moment? Well, a kurtosis value of 3 (don't worry about how that is calculated, it is beyond the scope of the exam) has zero kurtosis or no flatter or fatter tails than a symmetric normal distribution and a value less than 3 means the distribution is shorter and "pushes" more mass to the tails. By contrast, a value greater than 3 means a "taller" distribution, which "pulls" mass out of the tails and therefore has fewer extreme events than would be expected with a standard normal distribution.

It looks like Figure 2.

Figure 2: Coskewness and Cokurtosis

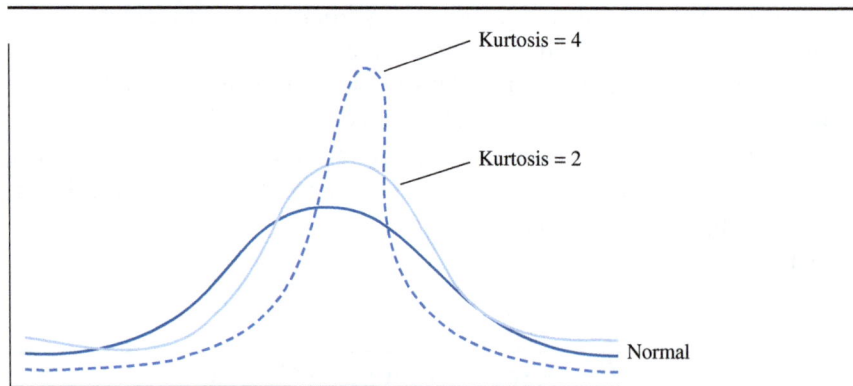

Think back to the idea of covariance and correlation. These describe how two random variables vary together, and coskewness and cokurtosis is exactly the same idea: How do higher moments of a distribution vary and change together?

It is possible for two portfolios to have the exact same mean and variance, but when combined with other portfolios with the exact same mean and variance the range of possible outcomes, to the downside or high-side, is very different.

The reading goes into quite a bit of detail of how to calculate these variables, but for the exam just know what they are, know they represent greater risk, and most analytic methods of risk calculation ignore them simply because, as we move beyond the second moment in a portfolio of any size, the correlation pairs can quickly climb into the millions. Essentially it is expensive to calculate.

Learning objective: Describe and interpret the best linear unbiased estimator.

If we look at all data points of a particular distribution we can get a population parameter—its mean, variance, or whatever we are looking for. Since we are looking at the entire population, we call this a parameter, not an estimator. For samples, we have only estimators of mean and variance—the best linear unbiased estimator (BLUE).

Taken one step further, we can calculate the mean and variance of estimators *themselves*. So the repeated measurement of a sample mean will return different estimators of the mean.

So the best unbiased estimator is one that has the least variance because we know that will be closest to the actual parameter value we are estimating the majority of the time.

Miller, Chapter 4

Michael Miller, *Mathematics and Statistics for Financial Risk Management*, 2nd Edition (Hoboken, NJ: John Wiley & Sons, 2013). Chapter 4. Distributions

After completing this reading you should be able to:

- Distinguish the key properties among the following distributions: uniform distribution, Bernoulli distribution, binomial distribution, Poisson distribution, normal distribution, lognormal distribution, chi-squared distribution, student's t distribution, and F-distribution, and identify common occurrences of each distribution.
- Describe the central limit theorem and the implications it has when combining i.i.d. random variables.
- Describe the properties of independent and identically distributed (i.i.d.) random variables.
- Describe a mixture distribution and explain the creation and characteristics of mixture distributions.

Learning objective: Distinguish the key properties among the following distributions: uniform distribution, Bernoulli distribution, binomial distribution, Poisson distribution, normal distribution, lognormal distribution, chi-squared distribution, student's t distribution, and F-distribution, and identify common occurrences of each distribution.

UNIFORM DISTRIBUTION

The uniform distribution is so called because its probability is uniform over some defined width and zero outside of that space.

It is a continuous distribution so its mean and variance do use integration, which makes it seem more complicated than it is. However, the uniform distribution does have use in approximating other more complex distributions, so it is worth knowing in the real world if not for the FRM exam.

Graphically the uniform distribution is shown in Figure 1.

Figure 1

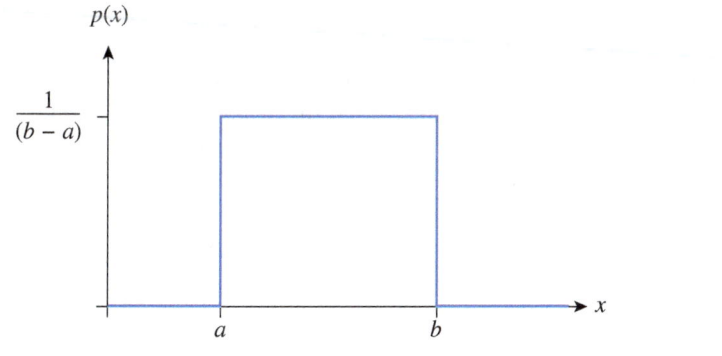

where the total area adds up to 1, as in any other probability distribution.

In this case if $b = 3$ and $a = 1$ $(b - a) = 2$. On the y axis we have $1/(3 - 1)$ because $2 \times 1/2 = 1$ and recovers the uniform measurement of 1.

If a were to equal 0 and $b = 1$, we would call this the standard uniform distribution, and this forms the basis of almost all numeric random number generators in finance.

BERNOULLI DISTRIBUTION

The most common representation of the Bernoulli distribution is a flip of a coin. This is most often used because the Bernoulli distribution is characterized by one distribution that has only one of two possible outcomes. This is usually expressed as a binary, meaning zero or one state, and a certain probability of each state, zero or one, is given. This distribution will become important very early on in derivatives pricing, especially in the construction of "trees" for option pricing. It will be the Bernoulli distribution that forms the foundation of the binomial tree, where we have a branching pattern that mimics the two possible future states from a starting state. The Bernoulli distribution is typically referred to in terms of probability p, with q being $1 - p$.

We can show this as:

$$\Pr(X = 1)$$
$$= 1 - \Pr(X = 0)$$
$$+ 1 - q = p$$

A **Bernoulli trial** is simply *an event or experiment that can be repeated, and that results in one of only two possible outcomes*. For instance, suppose you are betting on the movement of the price level of the stock market, and the two possible outcomes are either that it goes up or that it fails to go up (i.e., drops or stays the same). This can be seen as a Bernoulli trial that can be repeated each trading day. Your prediction may be correct or incorrect. If, on a given day, you correctly predict the direction on the market close, that result could be considered a successful Bernoulli trial.

Common occurrences: The Bernoulli distribution is commonly used in credit derivatives where the probability of default is estimated. In the case of default, a company either is or is not in bankruptcy. Therefore, the Bernoulli parameter that takes the form of zero or one representing whether or not the company is in bankruptcy is very useful for determining certain payoffs of credit derivatives. There may be dozens of other examples that are irrelevant for the FRM exam.

BINOMIAL DISTRIBUTION

The binomial distribution is a natural extension of the Bernoulli distribution and is the sum of many independent and identically Bernoulli-distributed random variables. The binomial distribution has a series of experiments with the outcome of some probability p and number of experiments n.

Since both the Bernoulli and the binomial distributions are discrete probability distributions—that is, they occur in discrete time—they are described by a probability mass function. For your own information, the probability mass function of the binomial distribution is as follows:

$$\Pr(X = x) = \binom{n}{x} p^k (1 = p)^{n-k}$$

$$\Pr(v > x) = Kx^{-a}$$

where

$$\binom{n}{x} = \frac{n!}{n!(n-x)!}$$

is read "N choose x".

Common occurrences: The binomial distribution can also be used in credit default swaps to price a basket of probability events, and more importantly, the binomial distribution is an important approximation to the normal when N is sufficiently large.

The accuracy of your prediction can be considered a discrete distribution, with an outcome of 1 if you are correct, and 0 if you are incorrect. Symbolically, a success could be denoted as $p(1) = P(X = 1)$. Suppose you have such skill that you are correct 60% of the time. We could then express the probability of your successful prediction as $p(1) = P(X = 1) = p = 0.60$. Therefore, the probability of failure is 0.40, which we can express as $p(0) = P(X = 0) = 1 - p = 1 - .60 = 0.40$.

Suppose you tried to predict the movement of the stock market each day for five days. Assume that each day is an independent trial, and that your probability of success does not vary from day to day. These predictions are five Bernoulli trials, and the number of successes you have in those five trials is a random variable (call it Y) that can be described by a binomial distribution.

$$P(r) = \frac{n!}{r!(n-r)!} p^r q^{n-r}$$

Where:

n = number of trials

r = number of observed successes

p = probability of success on each trial

q = probability of a failure, found by $1 - p$

! = factorial notation. $n!$ means the product of $n(n-1)(n-2)(n-3) \ldots (1)$. If $n = 4$, then $n! = (4)(3)(2)(1) = 24$. By definition, zero factorial, expressed 0!, is equal to 1.

Therefore, in our case:

$$P(3) \frac{5!}{3!(5-3)!} (0.60)^3 (0.40)^2 = \frac{120}{6 \times 2} (0.216)(0.16) = 0.3456$$

Interestingly, we see that there is less than a 35% chance we will get exactly three correct predictions out of five, even if our likelihood of success each time is equal to three out of five.

Find $P(0)$, $P(1)$, $P(2)$, $P(4)$, and $P(5)$. Using the formula above, you should get 1.024%, 7.68%, 23.04%, 25.92%, and 7.776%. Note that these, along with $P(3)$, add to 100%.

POISSON DISTRIBUTION

The Poisson distribution is sometimes described as the "arrival" distribution. This is because within queuing theory this describes how many cars, for example, arrive at a stoplight in a given period of time. The important information that we are looking for in this case is the probability of the number of events that are going to occur within a fixed period of time if we know the probability at which the events occur.

It is also an important aspect of a Poisson distribution to know that these events are independent of each other. Looking ahead toward derivatives pricing, the Poisson distribution begins to exhibit some of the memoryless properties of a Markovian process. Markovian processes are critical for understanding random walks, Brownian motion, geometric Brownian motion, and ultimately stochastic calculus.

The key thing to know for the FRM exam, however, is that the Poisson is a discrete distribution that describes the number of events that occur in a fixed time when these events are known to occur at some probability.

The probability mass function of Poisson looks like this:

$$f(j;\lambda) = \frac{\lambda j e^{-\lambda}}{j!}$$

In this case, j describes the number of events. Lamda (l) captures the expectation of the event and period of time. For example, if we knew that we expected a particular event to occur two times every five minutes and the time period that we were examining was 20 minutes, lambda would be set equal to eight. We arrive at this by taking the expectation of a number of events, two, and multiply that by the time. We are looking at 20 divided by 5 equals 4, which gives us a time period. Keep in mind this is all for your own information, and you will not be asked to explicitly calculate a Poisson distribution on the exam. This is very important in the real world, however.

The text at this point begins to introduce the idea of a "stochastic process." Stochastic is a fancy word for random, and that process is a mathematical expression. Therefore a stochastic process is a mathematical expression of randomness. The Poisson distribution is a generalization of a random process because of one key property that you know for the exam: That is, independent of when the last event occurred, the distribution of when the next event will occur is unaffected by the fact that it just happened.

This is a key distinction that is necessary to understand almost all of derivatives pricing. Later this property, called a Markovian process, is very important to begin thinking of how these discrete distributions can be extended to continuous time.

NORMAL DISTRIBUTION

Recall that since we are extending beyond discrete probability distributions and into the continuous realm, we move away from the idea of a probability mass function and into the idea of a probability density function. It is a key characteristic of all continuous functions that the probability of a single event is undefined. A continuous distribution is evaluating probabilities of events, not a discrete thing that occurs as a countable, individual event but as distribution of mass to describe the possibility of an event occurring over infinitesimally small intervals of time so we can always consider a smaller intervals of time. This is the idea between considering the 95% level of certainty and 99% level of certainty.

The probability density function of the standard normal is often written as:

$$\phi(x) = \frac{1}{\sqrt{2\pi}} e^{-\frac{1}{2}x^2}$$

where $\phi(x)$ is written as "fie (rhymes with pie) of x"

This is a special case of the normal distribution where $\mu = 0$, $\sigma^2 = 1$. In many cases the probability density function of the normal distribution is written as:

$$f(x) = \frac{1}{\sqrt{2\pi\sigma^2}} e^{\frac{-(x-\mu)^2}{2\sigma^2}}$$

You may see the distribution written both ways, and they are interchangeable.

LOGNORMAL DISTRIBUTION

One of the shortcomings of using the normal distribution for asset price modeling is that values of normally distributed random variables can fall below zero. Typically, asset values in the real world have a floor value of zero. The lognormal distribution does not have this problem, and consequently is a useful distribution for modeling the value of financial assets.

A random variable, say X, is considered lognormally distributed if its natural logarithm, ln(X), is normally distributed. The lognormal distribution is bound by zero at the left and has a long right tail (skewed right), without boundary.

The lognormal distribution is especially useful for modeling multiperiod, continuous compounding of asset returns. Recall that because of the central limit theorem, multiperiod asset returns can be described by the normal distribution, even when they are not normally distributed. Similarly, asset prices may not always be lognormally distributed, but the lognormal distribution still proves to be useful in various ways.

The mean and variance, respectively, of a lognormally distributed random variable are as follows:

$$\mu_L = e^{\left(\mu + 0.5\sigma^2\right)} \qquad \sigma_L^2 = e^{\left(2\mu + \sigma^2\right)}\left[e^{\sigma^2} - 1\right]$$

CHI-SQUARED (PRONOUNCED "KAI") DISTRIBUTION

The chi-squared distribution I think will be very important on the exam. What is a "chi" anyway? Chi is the 22nd letter of the Greek alphabet and in this case is used to describe the behavior of a random variable, which is the sum of normal random variables. This is a very widely used test for hypothesis testing, construction of confidence intervals, and more important, determining whether two random variables are truly independent.

The probability density function of the chi-squared distribution is given as:

$$f(x;k) = \frac{1}{2^{k/2}\Gamma(k/2)} x^{k/2-1} e^{-x/2} 1_{\{x \geq 0\}}$$

STUDENT'S T-DISTRIBUTION

Student's t-distribution will be the most important distribution for you on the exam. This is alternatively referred to as simply the "t" distribution and is a key distribution because it allows us to estimate the properties of a normal distribution when the sample size is small.

The key property is that the "t" distribution is used when the population standard deviation is unknown and has to be estimated from the sample. This is hugely important for both the exam and in the real world. So what the "t" distribution does is to allow you from a relatively small sample size for any population of an unknown variance to construct an estimation of the variance of the population as a whole. This is very important in the context of finance because it is almost impossible to choose from an entire population of data points that simply don't exist. The t-distribution will allow us to take samples of data points and construct appropriate estimations of the variances of the larger population as a whole.

One of the key characteristics of the t-distribution is that it differs from the normal distribution when plotted; the t-distribution is shorter and has fatter tails than the normal distribution. It should be clear that the normal distribution has extraordinarily thin tails, and almost in no circumstances will financial assets ever behave according to the normal distribution.

Therefore, the utilization of the normal distribution within the valuation process or risk estimation process is almost always flawed. This is fine if the limitations of the model and the assumptions of the model are well-understood and the implications of those limitations for valuation and pricing are also understood. However, this is almost never the case.

For the exam, make sure that you're comfortable knowing that the t-distribution should be used when the population variance is unknown, when the sample size is small, and that the visual difference between the t-distribution and the normal distribution is that the t-distribution has a shorter peak and fatter tails.

F-DISTRIBUTION

The chi-squared distribution is the distribution of sums of random variables and the F-distribution is the ratio of chi-squared distributions.

Why in the world would anyone want to do this? Suppose now we have two normally distributed random variables, each with their own means and variances, and we wish to test whether the population variances are the same. Knowing this distribution will enable us to construct a hypothesis test around the population variances of different samples.

Learning objective: Describe the central limit theorem and the implications it has when combining i.i.d. random variables.

The central limit theorem has some interesting features. Among them:

- Even if the population is not normally distributed, the sampling distribution will exhibit some of the characteristics of the normal distribution.
- If the population is normally distributed, the distribution of the sample means is also normally distributed.
- The mean of the sample means is equal to the population mean.
- The sampling distribution of the sample means has less dispersion—that is, a smaller standard deviation—than the population.
- This tendency toward the normal distribution is important and is the basis for the central limit theorem (CLT).

The central limit theorem states that if given a population characterized by any probability distribution (with mean μ and finite variance σ^2), the sampling distribution of the sample means (based on sample size n) will be approximately normally distributed with a mean of μ and variance σ^2/n, provided n is sufficiently large.

Three qualities of the CLT are very important:

- If the sample size is sufficiently large, the sampling distribution of sample means will be approximately normal. This is true whether the population is normally distributed or not (i.e., whether the population is normally distributed, skewed, or uniform, the theorem will apply.)
- The mean of the population, σ, and the mean of all possible sample means, σ, are equal. If the population is large and a large number of samples are selected from the population, then the mean of the sample means will be close to the population mean.
- There is no common agreement as to what "sufficiently large" means. Depending on how close the original population distribution is to normal, the minimal sample size may range from 10 to 30. The larger the sample size becomes, the better the properties above will hold. The law of large numbers says that the sample mean will be near the population mean when the sample size is high.

Learning objective: Describe the properties of independent and identically distributed (i.i.d.) random variables.

i.i.d. simply means *independently and identically distributed*. Take a sample from a barrel, make a note, and toss the sample back in. That is i.i.d.

The mean and variance of a sample average is an important topic on the FRM exam. Know first that a **population** *includes all objects or persons in a specific group being studied*. It is the set of all the observations for which we wish to draw conclusions.

A **sample** is *a subset of a population*.

Any measurable characteristic of a population, such as the mean, is called a **parameter**.

A parameter is a descriptive measure of a population. A **statistic** is a descriptive measure of a sample. Sample statistics are typically used to estimate population parameters.

Miller, Chapter 6

Michael Miller, *Mathematics and Statistics for Financial Risk Management*, 2nd Edition (Hoboken, NJ: John Wiley & Sons, 2013). Chapter 6. Bayesian Analysis (pp. 113–124 only)

After completing this reading you should be able to:

- Describe Bayes' theorem and apply this theorem in the calculation of conditional probabilities.
- Compare the Bayesian approach to the frequentist approach.
- Apply Bayes' theorem to scenarios with more than two possible outcomes and calculate posterior probabilities.

Learning objective: Describe Bayes' theorem and apply this theorem in the calculation of conditional probabilities.

Bayes' formula relates the conditional and marginal probabilities of two random events. Essentially, by using Bayes' formula, we can reverse the "given that probability" P(A|B) and convert it into P(B|A) using P(A) and P(B). Bear in mind that you will probably have to use the total probability rule to calculate P(A).

Replacing B with Event, and A with Information, Bayes' formula can be translated to:

$$P(Event\,|\,Information) = \frac{P(Information\,|\,Event) \times P(Event)}{P(Information)}$$

Example 1: Bayes' Formula

In a particular school, there are 54% boys and 46% girls. The girl students wear blue sweaters or red sweaters in equal numbers, while the boys all wear blue sweaters. An observer sees a (random) student from a distance, and all she can see is that the student is wearing a blue sweater. What is the probability that the student is a girl?

Solution

It is clear that the probability is less than 46% (the probability of the student being a girl), but by how much? Is it half that, because only half the girls wear blue sweaters? The correct answer can be computed using Bayes' theorem.

The event that we are interested in determining the probability of is that the student observed is a girl, and the information given is that the student observed is wearing a blue sweater. To compute P(B|A), we must determine:

- P(B): The unconditional probability that the student is a girl. This equals 0.46.
- P(B^c): The probability that the student is a boy (B^c is the complementary event to B). This equals 0.54.
- P(A|B): The probability of the student wearing a blue sweater given that the student is a girl. Girls are as likely to wear red sweaters as they are to wear blue

sweaters. Therefore, P(A|B) is 0.5. We can also calculate this as P(AB)/P(B). The joint probability of a student being a girl and wearing a blue sweater, P(AB), equals 0.23 (0.46 × 0.5), while the probability of a student being a girl, P(B), equals 0.46.

- $P(A | B^c)$: The probability of the student wearing a blue sweater given that the student is a boy. This is given as 1.
- P(A): The unconditional probability of a randomly selected student wearing a blue sweater. This can be calculated using the total probability rule:

$$P(A) = P(A|B) \times P(B) + P(A|B^c) \times P(B^c) = 0.5 \times 0.46 + 1 \times 0.54 = 0.77$$

Given all this information, the probability of the observer having spotted a girl given that the observed student is wearing a blue sweater can be computed as:

$$\begin{aligned} P(B|A) &= [P(A|B) \times P(B)] / P(A) \\ &= (0.5 \times 0.46) / 0.77 \\ &= 0.2987 \end{aligned}$$

As expected, the probability of a random student being a girl, given that he/she is wearing a blue sweater is less than 46%, but more than just half of 46%.

Another way to solve this problem is as follows: Assume that there are 100 students—54 boys and 46 girls. 54 boys and 23 girls wear blue sweaters. All together there are 77 blue sweater-wearers, of which 23 are girls. Therefore the chance that a random blue sweater-wearer is a girl equals 23/77 = 0.2987.

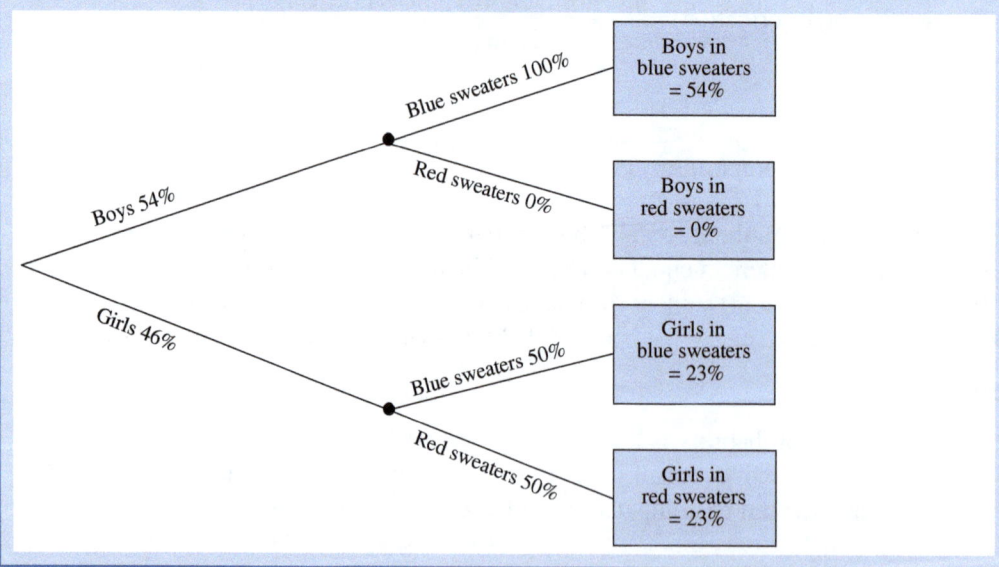

Learning objective: Compare the Bayesian approach to the frequentist approach.

The frequentist approach calculates probability of future events based on the frequency of prior positive events. The sun rises every morning with a sample size in the trillions. The probability of it rising tomorrow is as close to 100% as we can get. However, if we got heads on a coin toss with a sample size (frequency) of 1, we put very little faith in that result at all *if* we assume a fair coin. This is a prior assumption that is critical to Bayesian analysis that isn't required in the frequentist approach. What if we made a prior assumption that a coin was biased toward heads at 90%? Then that frequency of one event takes on much more meaning.

Basically, in the real world the shortcoming of Bayesian analysis is that we have to often make subjective assumptions about prior probabilities where the frequentist approach fails in small sample sizes. There are uses for both.

Learning objective: Apply Bayes' theorem to scenarios with more than two possible outcomes and calculate posterior probabilities.

A three- (or more) state Bayes' theorem calculation question is almost impossible to calculate by hand; notice this asks you just to "apply" so don't get bogged down in the examples in the assigned reading—they are unnecessary. In order to apply Bayes to scenarios with multiple states, we simply add extra "branches" to the earlier blue and red sweater example. In short, the application works exactly the same way but you don't need to worry about how to calculate it on the exam—so don't worry, because it is a brutal calculation.

Miller, Chapter 7

Michael Miller, *Mathematics and Statistics for Financial Risk Management,* 2nd Edition (Hoboken, NJ: John Wiley & Sons, 2013). Chapter 7. Hypothesis Testing and Confidence Intervals

After completing this reading you should be able to:

- Calculate and interpret the sample mean and sample variance.
- Construct and interpret a confidence interval.
- Construct an appropriate null and alternative hypothesis, and calculate an appropriate test statistic.
- Differentiate between a one-tailed and a two-tailed test and identify when to use each test.
- Interpret the results of hypothesis tests with a specific level of confidence.
- Demonstrate the process of backtesting VaR by calculating the number of exceedances.

Learning objective: Calculate and interpret the sample mean and sample variance.

Often we choose a sample from the population in order to learn something about a specific characteristic of the population. An example would be selecting a sample of European stocks to include in a measure of the average ROE of European equities, rather than including all European stocks, some of which may be very small and unrepresentative of the European market.

The sample mean is the same as the arithmetic mean; it is an arithmetic average.

Any measurable characteristic of a sample, such as the sample mean, is called a **statistic**.

For example, suppose that in a study of 65 U.S. equity issues with multiple restructuring charges in the previous five years, 35 were found to have had two restructuring charges, 25 had three restructuring charges, and 5 had four restructuring charges:

The **sample mean** is *the sum of all the values in the sample divided by the total number of values in the sample*:

The sample variance is just the same thing—the variance of the sample we have chosen and is an estimator of the population variance:

$$s^2 = \frac{\sum (X - \bar{X})^2}{n - 1}$$

Where:

s^2 = represents the sample variance

X = value of the observations in the sample

$\bar{X}$ = mean of the sample

n = total number of observations in the sample

Using $n-1$ instead of n in the denominator of the sample variance is a correction that reflects the fact that the sample mean, rather than the population mean, is being used in calculating the sample variance. If n were used, the sample variance would be a biased estimate of the population variance (the variance would be underestimated). This can become a serious bias when the sample size is small.

For example, suppose a group of Internet service providers have the following revenue-per-member: 20, 40, 25, 45, and 15. The sample variance, which estimates the population variance, is:

$$s^2 = \frac{\sum (X - \bar{X})^2}{n-1} = \frac{670}{5-1} = 167.5$$

Learning objective: Construct and interpret a confidence interval.

I can almost guarantee that you'll be asked about confidence intervals on the exam. Either in a hypothesis test question or a pure calculation. You need to be very comfortable with these ideas. The key to setting up a confidence interval is to define the critical values at which you are testing and put the properties of the random variable in between those two key statistics.

*The **confidence interval** is the range of values derived from sample data such that the population parameter occurs within that range with a specified probability.* For example, the confidence interval for the population mean is the interval that has a probability equal to $1 - \alpha$ (where α is small) of containing the population mean, m. The two most common confidence intervals used are the 95% and 99% confidence intervals. *The value $1 - \alpha$ is referred to as the **degree of confidence**.*

A 95% confidence interval means that about 95% of the similarly constructed intervals contain the parameter being estimated. If we use the 99% level of confidence, then we expect about 99% of the intervals to contain the parameter being estimated.

If the parameter we are estimating is normally distributed, then another interpretation of the 95% confidence interval is that 95% of the sample means for a specified sample size will lie within 1.96 standard deviations of the population mean. Similarly, for the 99% confidence interval, 99% of the sample means will lie within 2.575 standard deviations of the population mean.

How do we get 1.96 and 2.575? Because the sample mean is normally distributed (according to the central limit theorem) we can use the normal distribution curve. The middle 95% of the sample means lie equally on either side of the mean, so logically, 95%/2 = .4750 or 47.50%. Thus, the area to each side of the mean is .4750. We add 0.5 to this value, to obtain 0.9750, and look that value up in Appendix A. We find that the *z*-value to the right of the mean is +1.96, and the *z*-value to the left is –1.96. The same procedure can be done to find the *z*-value of 2.575.

To construct a confidence interval, we first need to compute the **standard error of the sample means,** *which is the standard deviation of the sampling distribution of the sample means.*

To understand the concept of degrees of freedom, we can examine the calculation of the sample variance.

When calculating the unbiased estimator of the sample variance that we use:

$$s_X^2 = \frac{\sum (X_i - \bar{X})^2}{n-1}$$

The term in the denominator, $n-1$, which is the sample size minus 1, is the number of degrees of freedom in estimating the population variance. We also use $n-1$ as the number of degrees of freedom for determining reliability factors based on the *t*-distribution. The term *degrees of freedom* is used because in a random sample, we assume that observations are selected independently of each other. The numerator of the sample variance, however, has used the sample mean already, which is calculated from the same sample itself.

How would this added calculation on the numerator affect the number of observations that are collected independently for the sample variance formula? For example, with a sample of size 20 and a mean of 10%, you can freely select only 19 additional observations if you already used the sample mean in the numerator. Given the 19 observations, you can always find the value for the 20th observation, so that the mean equals 10%. So in terms of the sample variance formula, you only have 19 degrees of freedom after you have used the sample mean in the numerator.

In other words, given that you must first compute the sample mean from the total of n independent observations, only $n-1$ observations can be chosen independently for the calculation of the sample variance. The concept of degrees of freedom comes up frequently in statistics, and you will see it often in later sections.

Upon obtaining a point estimate, we often wish to quantify how close we think our point estimate is likely to be to the population parameter it is estimating. This is especially true if the underlying distribution is unknown *and* the sample size yielding that point estimate is small. To quantify our confidence, we construct a confidence interval around our point estimate.

The steps toward construction of confidence intervals are normally the following:

- Obtain the point estimate of the examined parameter.
- Calculate the standard error (via the standard deviation and number of observations).
- Identify the appropriate critical value (also known as critical or reliability factor) based on the **assumed underlying distribution** and desired **level of confidence**.

When n is greater than 30, it is generally considered that the sample is "large" and therefore the central limit theorem applies fairly well. We can then construct the confidence intervals for the population mean μ using the standard normal distribution as follows:

90% confidence interval: $\bar{X} \pm 1.645 \dfrac{s}{\sqrt{n}}$

95% confidence interval: $\bar{X} \pm 1.960 \dfrac{s}{\sqrt{n}}$

99% confidence interval: $\bar{X} \pm 2.575 \dfrac{s}{\sqrt{n}}$

Learning objective: Construct an appropriate null and alternative hypothesis, and calculate an appropriate test statistic.

Hypothesis testing is the process of evaluating the accuracy of a statement regarding a population parameter (e.g., the population mean) given sample information (e.g., the sample mean). A hypothesis is a statement about the value of a population parameter developed for the purpose of testing a theory. Let's assume that we think (hypothesize) that the average points scored in each game by a basketball player throughout his career is greater than 30.

First, we would need to get some sample information. Then we would conduct a hypothesis test on the sample information (average of his scores in, let's say, 49 randomly selected games) in order to be able to comment on the accuracy of the statement pertaining to the population parameter (his average score across all the games that he played in his entire career).

1. The null hypothesis (H_0) generally represents the status quo, and is the hypothesis that we are interested in rejecting. This hypothesis will not be rejected unless the sample data provides sufficient evidence to reject it. Null hypotheses regarding the mean of the population can be stated in the following ways:

   $H_0: \mu \leq \mu_0$

   $H_0: \mu \geq \mu_0$

   $H_0: \mu = \mu_0$

   where:
   μ = population mean
   μ_0 = hypothesized value of the population mean

   In the basketball player's example that we just described, the null hypotheses would be that the player's average score is less than or equal to 30 points. Confirmation of our belief (that his average score is greater than 30) requires rejection of the null hypothesis.

2. The alternate hypothesis (H_a) is essentially the statement whose validity we are trying to evaluate. The alternate hypothesis is the statement that will be accepted only if the sample data provides convincing evidence of its truth. It is the conclusion of the test if the null hypothesis is rejected. Alternate hypotheses can be stated as:

   $H_a: \mu > \mu_0$

   $H_a: \mu < \mu_0$

   $H_a: \mu \neq \mu_0$

In our example, the alternate hypothesis is that the player's scoring average is greater than 30 points. Recall that we are trying to evaluate the validity of the statement that his scoring average is greater than 30 points.

A hypothesis test is always conducted at a particular level of significance (α). The level of significance represents the chance that we are willing to take that the conclusion from the test might be wrong.

Essentially, a hypothesis test involves the comparison of a sample's test statistic to a critical value.

- The test statistic is calculated as:

$$\text{Test statistic} = \frac{\text{Sample statistic} - \text{Hypothesized value}}{\text{Standard error of sample statistic}}$$

- The critical value depends on the relevant distribution, sample size, and level of significance used to test the hypothesis.

Learning objective: Differentiate between a one-tailed and a two-tailed test and identify when to use each test.

ONE-TAILED TESTS

When the region of rejection is only on one tail of the curve, it indicates that a **one-tailed test** is being applied.

The test is a one-tailed test if H_1 states a direction (stating either "greater than" or "less than"), such as µ > or µ <.

To illustrate, suppose:

H_0: 354, which reads "the population mean is less than or equal to 354."

H_1: 354, which reads "the population mean is greater than 354."

A clever way to determine the location of the rejection region is to look at the direction in which the inequality is pointing in the alternate hypothesis. If it is pointing to the right, the rejection region is on the right; the converse is true if it points left. If there is no inequality sign in the alternate hypothesis, the test is two-tailed.

If no direction is specified under the alternate hypothesis, H_1, a **two-tailed test** is being applied.

> **Example 1: One-Tailed Hypothesis Test**
>
> Suppose that the basketball player's average score in a sample of 49 games is 36 points with a standard deviation of 9 points. Determine the accuracy of the statement that his career scoring average is greater than 30 points. Use the 5% level of significance.
>
> **Solution**
>
> The null hypothesis is the statement that we want to reject (that his average score is less than or equal to 30), and the alternate hypothesis is the belief whose validity we are trying to ascertain (that his average is greater than 30).

Therefore:

$H_0: \mu \leq 30 \rightarrow$ The theory that we want to reject
$H_a: \mu > 30 \rightarrow$ The theory that we want to validate

The observed sample's test statistic (z-score) represents the number of standard deviations away from the hypothesized mean the sample's mean lies.

$$\text{Test statistic} = \frac{\text{Sample statistic} - \text{Hypothesized value}}{\text{Standard error of sample statistic}}$$

$$\text{Test statistic} = \frac{\bar{x} - \mu_0}{s/\sqrt{n}} = \frac{36 - 30}{(9/\sqrt{49})} = 4.67$$

The critical value at the 5% significance level tells us the number of standard deviations away from the hypothesized mean, only 5% of observed sample means lie.

$$\text{Critical value} = Z_\alpha = 1.645$$

The test statistic indicates that the sample mean (36) lies 4.67 standard errors, or standard deviations of the sampling distribution, away from the hypothesized mean (30). Therefore, it lies in the region where less than 5% of observed sample means lie. There is a less than 5% chance of observing a sample mean as high as 36 (given the sample size of 49 and a sample standard deviation of 9), if the population mean is 30. Therefore, at the 5% significance level, we can *reject* the null hypothesis, and conclude that the player's scoring average across his entire career is greater than 30.

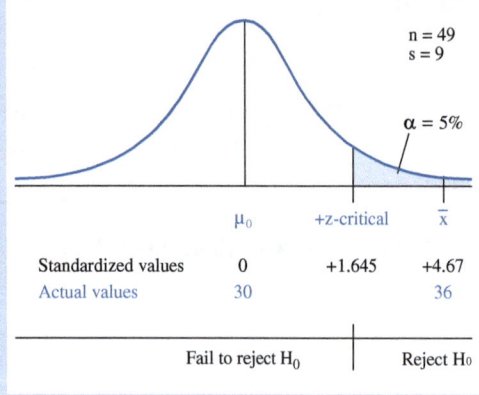

5% of observed sample means lie more than 1.645 standard deviations above the mean.

The test statistic lies 4.67 standard deviations above the mean.

The chance of a sample having a mean of 36 (given the sample size of 49 and sample standard deviation of 9), when the population mean equals 30 is less than 5%. Therefore we **reject the null hypothesis.**

The following rejection rules apply when trying to determine whether a population mean is greater than the hypothesized value.

- Reject H_0 when:

    Test statistic > positive critical value

- Fail to reject H_0 when:

    Test statistic ≤ positive critical value

Example 2: One-Tailed Hypothesis Test

For the same data that we used in the previous example, assume that the sample has a mean of 28.5. Evaluate the validity of the statement that the player's scoring average over his career is less than 30 points at the 5% level of significance.

Solution

In this case, we want to reject the theory that his average score is greater than or equal to 30 and test the validity of the claim that his average score is less than 30.

Therefore,

$H_0 : \mu \geq 30 \rightarrow$ The theory that we want to reject
$H_a : \mu < 30 \rightarrow$ The theory that we want to validate

$$\text{Critical value} = -Z_\alpha = -1.645$$

The sample's test statistic (z-score) represents the number of standard deviations that the observed sample mean lies away from the hypothesized mean. For the information we are given, the observed sample mean (28.5) lies 1.167 standard deviations *below* the hypothesized mean of 30.

$$\text{Test statistic} = \frac{\bar{x} - \mu_0}{s/\sqrt{n}} = \frac{28.5 - 30}{(9/\sqrt{49})} = 1.167$$

The critical value (−1.645) tells us the number of standard deviations *below* the mean, only 5% of observed sample means lie. The test statistic (1.167) lies *less* than 1.645 standard deviations *below* the mean. The sample mean lies close enough to the hypothesized mean for us not to be able to reject the null hypothesis. Therefore, at the 5% significance level, we fail to reject the null hypothesis.

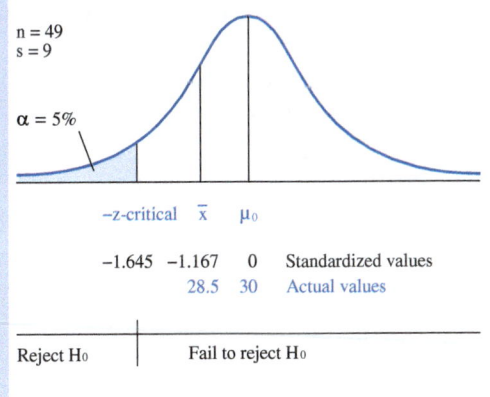

5% of observed sample means lie more than 1.645 standard deviations *below* the mean.

The test statistic only lies 1.167 standard deviations *below* the mean.

The chance of a sample (given the sample size of 49 and sample standard deviation of 9) having a mean of 28.5 when the population mean equals 30 is more than 5%. Therefore we **fail to reject the null hypothesis** at the 5% significance level.

The following rejection rules apply when trying to determine whether a population mean is greater than the hypothesized value.

- Reject H_0 when:

    Test statistic < negative critical value

- Fail to reject H_0 when:

    Test statistic ≥ negative critical value

Under two-tailed tests, we assess whether the value of the population parameter is simply different from a given hypothesized value. The hypotheses for two-tailed tests are stated as:

$$H_0 : \mu = \mu_0$$
$$H_a : \mu \neq \mu_0$$

Two-tailed hypotheses tests have two rejection regions. Example 3 illustrates how two-tailed hypotheses tests are performed.

Example 3: Two-Tailed Hypothesis Test

A **two-tailed test** will be used to determine if the player's scoring average is simply different from, or not equal to 30. His scores can differ from 30 in two ways—by being *less* than 30 or by being *more* than 30: hence the two-tailed test. Given that over a sample of 49 games, the player averaged 33 points with a standard deviation of 9 points, test whether his career scoring average is different from 30 at the 5% significance level.

$H_0 : \mu = 30 \rightarrow$ The theory that we want to reject
$H_a : \mu \neq 30 \rightarrow$ The theory that we want to validate

$$\text{Test statistic} = \frac{\bar{x} - \mu_0}{s/\sqrt{n}} = \frac{33 - 30}{(9/\sqrt{49})} = 2.33$$

At the α level of significance, we want to determine whether the sample mean lies within $Z_{\alpha/2}$ standard deviations from the hypothesized population mean. This leaves a combined probability of α in the tails.

Critical value $= -Z_{\alpha/2} = -1.96$ and $+1.96$

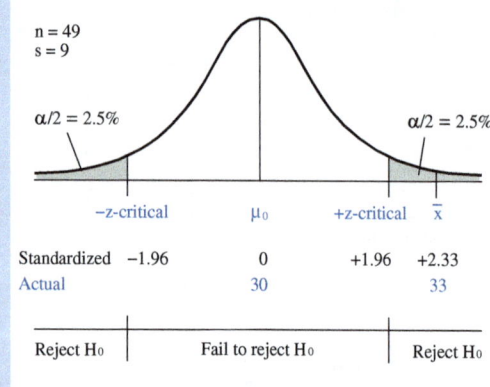

5% of observed sample means lie more than 1.96 standard deviations away from the mean, i.e., 2.5% in each tail.

The test statistic lies 2.33 standard deviations *above* the mean.

The chance of a sample having a mean of 33 (given the sample size of 49 and sample standard deviation of 9) when the population mean equals 30 is less than 2.5%. Therefore **we reject the null hypothesis.**

At the 5% level of significance, the sample mean must lie within 1.96 standard deviations of the hypothesized population mean for the null hypothesis to not be rejected. If the sample mean lies beyond either 1.96 standard deviations above the mean or 1.96 standard deviations below the mean, we cannot conclude that the population mean equals the hypothesized value, and have to reject the null hypothesis. In this example, our test statistic (2.33) lies more than 1.96 standard deviations above the mean.

The chances of a sample mean actually representing the population mean while lying so far away from the population mean (2.33 standard deviations) are extremely slim (less than

5%). Therefore, we reject the null hypothesis, and conclude that the player's career scoring average is not equal to 30 at the 5% significance level.

REJECTION RULES FOR TWO-TAILED HYPOTHESIS TEST

- Reject H_0 when:

  Test statistic < Lower critical value

  Test statistic > Upper critical value

- Fail to reject H_0 when:

  Lower critical value ≤ test statistic ≤ Upper critical value

Notice that in all the examples above we have been very careful to word the conclusions that we have drawn from the hypothesis tests. The conclusion of any hypothesis test is either the rejection of the null, or failure to reject the null. For example, we cannot make a statement like "the null hypothesis is accepted" because it is statistically incorrect to do so.

Learning objective: Interpret the results of hypothesis tests with a specific level of confidence.

$$\left[\begin{pmatrix}\text{sample}\\\text{statistic}\end{pmatrix} - \begin{pmatrix}\text{critical}\\\text{value}\end{pmatrix}\begin{pmatrix}\text{standard}\\\text{error}\end{pmatrix}\right] \leq \begin{pmatrix}\text{population}\\\text{parameter}\end{pmatrix} \leq \left[\begin{pmatrix}\text{sample}\\\text{statistic}\end{pmatrix} + \begin{pmatrix}\text{critical}\\\text{value}\end{pmatrix}\begin{pmatrix}\text{standard}\\\text{error}\end{pmatrix}\right]$$

$$\bar{X} - (z_{\alpha/2})(s/\sqrt{n}) \leq \mu_0 \leq \bar{X} + (z_{\alpha/2})(s/\sqrt{n})$$

As you can see, we reach the same conclusion regarding our hypothesis using a hypothesis test or using confidence intervals. Confidence intervals and hypothesis tests are linked by critical values.

- In a confidence interval, we aim to determine whether the hypothesized value of the population mean (μ_0), lies within a computed interval with a particular degree of confidence ($1 - \alpha$). Here the interval represents the "fail-to-reject-the-null region" and is based around, or centered on the sample mean, x.
- In a hypothesis test, we examine whether the sample mean, x lies in the rejection region (i.e., outside the interval) or in the fail-to-reject-the-null region (i.e., within the interval) at a particular level of significance (α). Here the interval is based around, or centered on, the hypothesized value of the population mean (μ_0).

Figure 1: A 95% Confidence Interval for a Two-Tailed Test

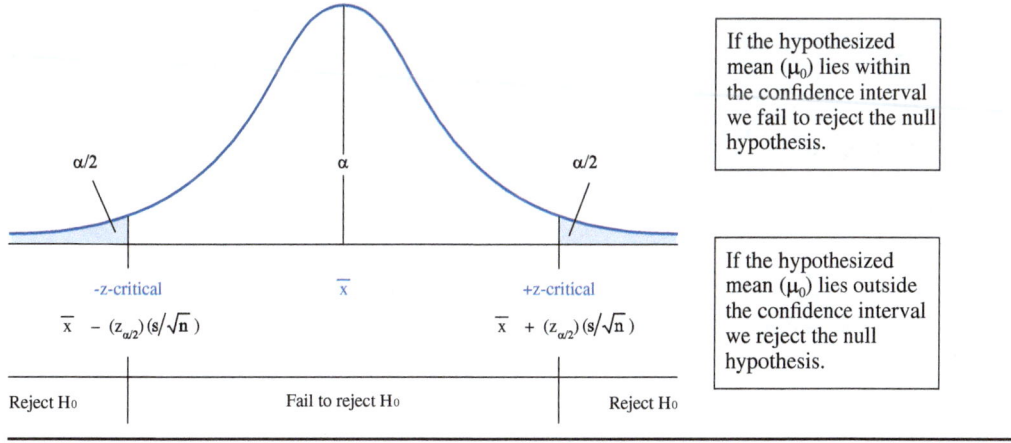

Example 4: Confidence Intervals

Construct a 95% confidence interval for the basketball player's career scoring average if, over a sample of 49 games, he averaged 31 points with a standard deviation of 9 points. Use this confidence interval to determine whether the player's career average is different from 33 points.

Solution

$$\bar{x} - (z_{\alpha/2})(s/\sqrt{n}) \leq \mu_0 \leq \bar{x} + (z_{\alpha/2})(s/\sqrt{n})$$

Critical value = $Z_{\alpha/2} = Z_{0.025} = 1.96$

Sample mean = $\bar{x} = 31$

$$31 - 1.96 \times \left(\frac{9}{\sqrt{49}}\right) \leq \text{career scoring average} \leq 31 + 1.96 \times \left(\frac{9}{\sqrt{49}}\right)$$

$28.48 \leq$ career scoring average (hypothesized population mean, μ_0) ≤ 33.52

There is a 95% probability that the population mean lies within this interval given the sample mean of 31 points. The hypothesized population mean (33) lies within this range. Therefore, we fail to reject the null hypothesis at the 5% level of significance.

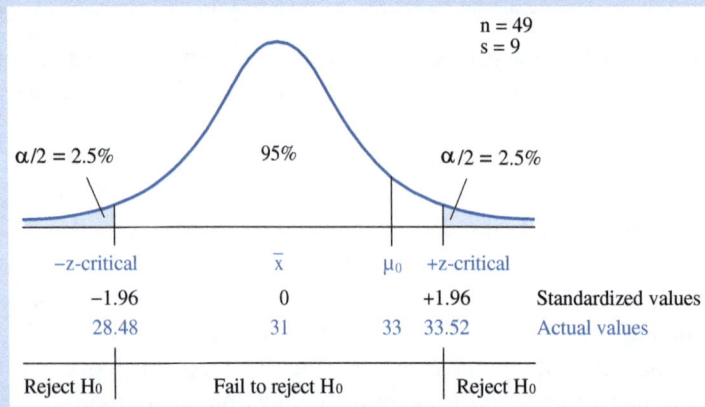

Conducting a hypothesis test would also lead us to the same conclusion:

$H_0 : \mu = 33$
$H_a : \mu \neq 33$

$$\text{Test statistic} = \frac{\bar{x} - \mu_0}{s/\sqrt{n}} = \frac{31 - 33}{(9/\sqrt{49})} = -1.556$$

The critical z-values at the 5% level of significance are –1.96 and +1.96. The test statistic (1.556) falls in the range between these two values. Therefore, we fail to reject the null hypothesis at the 5% level of significance. Note that both the confidence interval and the hypothesis test offer the same conclusion.

Learning objective: Demonstrate the process of backtesting VaR by calculating the number of exceedances.

Backtesting means taking a model and seeing how it would perform given actual, historical data. With VaR, this is an important test to make sure if we had been using that particular model, our risk exceedances—a day we actually exceeded the loss the VaR model said we would—matches actual exceedances experienced on that day.

The reason backtesting is necessary is because the more we move into higher degrees of certainty, say 99.99%, we are unsure of the actual shape of the distribution that far into extreme events.

You may think, "Isn't the whole idea of a distribution that we know exactly what its shape, and therefore the probability (area under the curve at that point), actually is?" That is true about the nature of the distribution itself, but we also know that the real world doesn't behave according to the shape of the normal distribution—especially in the tail—so by backtesting and observing exceedances compared to historic data, we can see if our model throws off too many—or too few—days where our risk limits would have been exceeded.

STOCK, CHAPTER 4

James Stock and Mark Watson, Introduction to Econometrics, Brief Edition (Boston: Pearson Education, 2008). Chapter 4. Linear Regression with One Regressor

After completing this reading you should be able to:

- Explain how regression analysis in econometrics measures the relationship between dependent and independent variables.
- Interpret a population regression function, regression coefficients, parameters, slope, intercept, and the error term.
- Interpret a sample regression function, regression coefficients, parameters, slope, intercept, and the error term.
- Describe the key properties of a linear regression.
- Define an ordinary least squares (OLS) regression and calculate the intercept and slope of the regression.
- Describe the method and three key assumptions of OLS for estimation of parameters.
- Summarize the benefits of using OLS estimators.
- Describe the properties of OLS estimators and their sampling distributions, and explain the properties of consistent estimators in general.
- Interpret the explained sum of squares, the total sum of squares, the residual sum of squares, the standard error of the regression, and the regression R_2.
- Interpret the results of an OLS regression.

Learning objective: Explain how regression analysis in econometrics measures the relationship between dependent and independent variables.

This statement is quite basic and most likely not going to be tested directly on the exam. The key idea here is that typically Y represents the dependent variable and X the independent variable. The real idea in econometrics is that there is some related, economic theory that justifies the relationship between the two random variables being chosen.

It's also important to recognize where spurious correlation comes in. For example, one could potentially chart two random variables X and Y and notice that they are almost perfectly correlated. This perfect correlation or one-to-one relationship is identified by a slope of the regression line at a 45° angle. However, if one random variable is rainfall in Detroit, and the other random variable is gasoline sold in Florida, we can reasonably assume that those two things are actually unrelated and therefore we are seeing a spurious correlation within the regression analysis.

The key takeaway for the exam is that correlation is not causation. While this is a very simple idea within the context of risk management, it is very important as we'll see later because correlation becomes increasingly important later on. Things that seem to be uncorrelated in times of normal market behavior suddenly become correlated in times of stress.

It is this changing correlation dynamic that linear regression simply will not capture.

> **Learning objective: Interpret a population regression function, regression coefficients, parameters, slope, intercept, and the error term.**

Linear regression is used to summarize the relationship between two variables that are linearly related. It is used to make predictions about a dependent variable, Y (also known as the explained variable, endogenous variable, and predicted variable) using an independent variable, X (also known as the explanatory variable, exogenous variable, and predicting variable), to test hypotheses regarding the relation between the two variables, and to evaluate the strength of the relationship between them.

The dependent variable is the variable whose variation we are seeking to explain, while the independent variable is the variable that is used to explain the variation in the dependent variable.

> **Regression model equation** = $Y_i = b_0 + b_1 X_i + \varepsilon_i,\ i = 1,...., n$

where:

- b_1 and b_0 are the regression coefficients.
- b_1 is the slope coefficient.
- b_0 is the intercept term.
- ε is the error term that represents the variation in the dependent variable that is not explained by the independent variable.

In order to calculate a confidence interval, we first have to calculate the regression coefficients. Based on this model, the regression process estimates the line of best fit for the data in the sample. The regression line takes the following form:

> **Regression line equation** = $\hat{Y}_i = \hat{b}_0 + \hat{b}_1 X_i,\ i = 1,..., n$

Linear regression computes the line of best fit that minimizes the sum of the squared regression residuals (the squared vertical distances between actual observations of the dependent variable and the regression line). What this means is that it looks to obtain estimates, $\hat{b}_0$ and $\hat{b}_1$, for b_0 and b_1 respectively, that minimize the sum of the squared differences between the actual values Y, Y_i, and the predicted values of Y, $\hat{Y}_i$, according to the regression equation ($\hat{Y}_i = \hat{b}_0 + \hat{b}_1 X_i$).

When graphed, our regression looks like Figure 1.

Figure 1: Regression Line and Scatter Plot

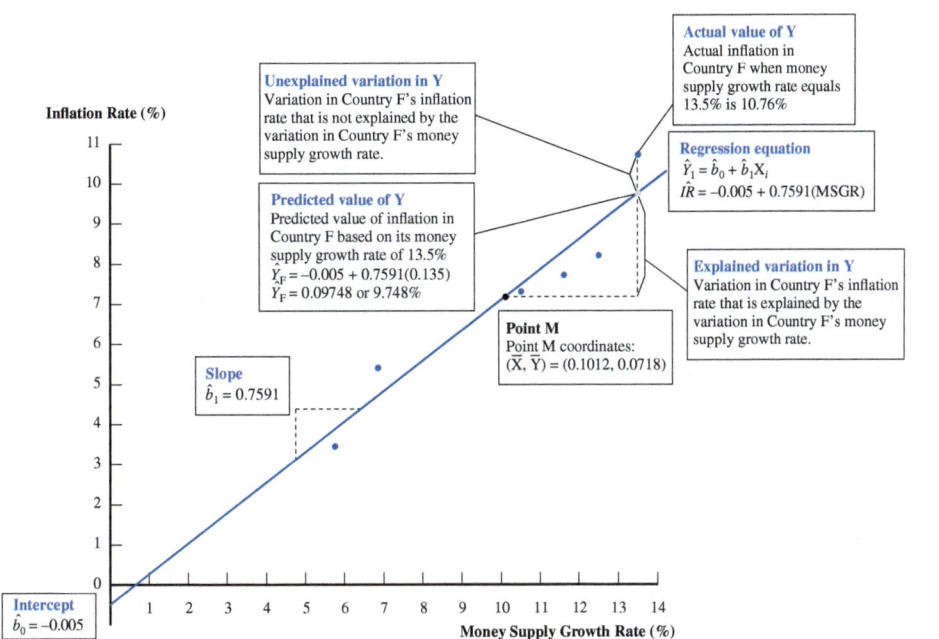

Learning objective: Interpret a sample regression function, regression coefficients, parameters, slope, intercept, and the error term.

This is best done with an example. Consider this interpretation of the relationship among money supply growth and inflation.

Determine the slope coefficient and the intercept term of a simple linear regression using money supply growth as the independent variable and the inflation rate as the dependent variable. See Example 1.

> ### Example 1: Linear Regression
>
> For the money supply growth and inflation rate data that we have been working with in this reading, determine the slope coefficient and the intercept term of a simple linear regression using money supply growth as the independent variable and the inflation rate as the dependent variable. The data provided below is excerpted from Example 2:
>
> | Country | Money Supply Growth Rate (X_i) | Inflation Rate (Y_i) | Cross Product $(X_i - \bar{X})(Y_i - \bar{Y})$ | Squared Deviations $(X_i - \bar{X})^2$ | Squared Deviations $(Y_i - \bar{Y})^2$ |
> |---|---|---|---|---|---|
> | Sum | 0.607 | 0.4306 | 0.003735 | 0.004921 | 0.003094 |
> | Average | 0.1012 | 0.0718 | | | |
> | Covariance | | | 0.000747 | | |
> | Variance | | | | 0.000984 | 0.000619 |
> | Std. Dev (s) | | | | 0.031373 | 0.024874 |

Solution

The regression equation can be stated as:

Inflation rate = $b_0 + b_1$ (Money supply growth rate) + ε

Typically, regression software is used to determine the regression coefficients. However, for illustrative purposes we perform the calculations to make the source of the numbers clear.

Slope coefficient = $\hat{b}_1$ = Cov (X, Y)/Var(X) = 0.000747/0.000984 = 0.7591

Note that the slope coefficient can be computed in this manner only when there is one independent variable.

In a linear regression, the regression line passes through the coordinates corresponding to the mean values of the independent and dependent variables. Using the mean values for money supply growth ($\bar{X}$ = 0.1012) and the inflation rate ($\bar{Y}$ = 0.0718) we can compute the intercept term as:

$$\bar{Y} = \hat{b}_0 + \hat{b}_1 \bar{X}$$

$\hat{b}_0$ = 0.0718 − (0.7591)(0.1012) = −0.005

Therefore, the relationship between the money supply growth rate and the inflation rate for our sample data can be expressed as:

Inflation rate = −0.005 + 0.7591 (Money supply growth rate)

The regression equation implies that:

- For every 1-percentage-point increase in the money supply growth rate, the inflation rate is predicted to increase by 0.7591 percentage points. The slope coefficient ($\hat{b}_1$) is interpreted as the estimated change in the dependent variable for a 1-unit change in the independent variable.
- If the money supply growth rate in a country equals 0, the inflation rate in the country will be −0.5%. The intercept ($\hat{b}_0$) is an estimate of the dependent variable when the independent variable equals 0.

Learning objective: Describe the key properties of a linear regression.

1. The relationship between the dependent variable (Y) and the independent variable (X) is linear in the parameters, b_1 and b_0. This means that b_1 and b_0 are raised to the first power only and neither of them is multiplied or divided by another regression parameter.
2. The independent variable, X, is not random.
3. The expected value of the error term is zero: $E(\varepsilon) = 0$.
4. The variance of the error term is constant for all observations. This is known as the homoskedasticity assumption.
5. The error term is uncorrelated across observations.
6. The error term is normally distributed.

Learning objective: Define an ordinary least squares (OLS) regression and calculate the intercept and slope of the regression.

Keep in mind that this is a "describe" learning objective. It is very easy to get wrapped up in the mass and the sigma notation to the ordinary least squares. Stay focused on what the question is actually asking you and you'll save yourself a lot of headache for the exam.

Just as in statistics, we have the sample and the population. In regression analysis, this is called the sample regression function and the population regression function. The ordinary least squares seeks to minimize the error term and therefore provides the best estimation of parameters in order to provide the best explanation of the relationship.

It is important to note that we are not observing the entire population (the population regression function) but rather the sample regression function, since in reality we will only have a sample of the population and not the entire population.

The ordinary least squares method says that the parameters of the slope and intercept should be minimized in a way that the residual sum of squares is minimized.

In this case residual is referring to the error term; in this case we're using the letter u. The Sigma notation means that we are going to take the sum of the squared error terms. The reason that we take the error terms to the second power is not immediately obvious, but imagine if you had an error term that alternated between +3 and −3. It would appear that this linear regression, if we were simply to sum the error terms, had an error term of zero, but that's clearly not the case. So by squaring the error terms we remove the impact of the sign and we preserve the variation of the error term. This is exactly what the residual sum of squares refers to.

The next step in describing what an ordinary least squares means is visually showing what it would mean to have no error term. Remember that the error term expresses the difference between the actual observed value minus the expected value of the value that is predicted by the regression equation, or more importantly the conditional expectation or conditional probability. All of these terms are closely related. So mathematically we can express the error term as the difference between the observed value minus the expected value (mean) as follows:

$$ESS = \sum_{i=1}^{n} \left(\hat{Y}_i - \bar{Y} \right)^2$$

All we are seeing here is that we are adding up all of the observed Y values minus the expected value of Y and we are squaring it. We are simply transforming the lower case u which describes the sum of all possible errors and we're breaking out what you actually see.

The error term is the difference between the observed value of the random variable minus what we expect that random variable to be, based on the regression equation we are using. We are then taking that to the second power to minimize or actually to eliminate the impact of a positive or negative difference from the regression equation.

In summary: The ordinary least squares methodology seeks to minimize the square of the error term. We square the error term to remove the impact of both positive and negative variation away from the regression line. Since we are seeking to minimize the error term among all points of data, we use sigma notation. So the foundation of ordinary least squares squared is the residual sum of squares.

We can further break down the expected value of Y in terms of the parameters of the linear regression equation. We seek to minimize the error term by manipulating both the slope coefficient and the intercept. Once we have minimized this, this equation is the best fit for the data we have. Best fit in this case is defined as a regression equation whose error term is minimized.

To further unify this idea of OLS, we are going to refer to this example a number of times in this chapter. Be very sure you understand how all these parts work together because you will see this on exam day.

$$\text{Sample variance} = s_X^2 = \sum_{i=1}^{n}(X_i - \overline{X})^2 / (n-1)$$

$$\text{Sample standard deviation} = s_X = \sqrt{s_X^2}$$

Example 2: Using Ordinary Least Squared

Using the money supply growth and inflation data from 1990 to 2010 for the 6 countries in Example 2 calculate the covariance and the correlation coefficient.

Solution:

Country	Money Supply Growth Rate (X_i)	Inflation Rate (Y_i)	Cross Product $(X_i - \overline{X})(Y_i - \overline{Y})$	Squared Deviations $(X_i - \overline{X})^2$	Squared Deviations $(Y_i - \overline{Y})^2$
A	0.0685	0.0545	0.000564	0.001067	0.000298
B	0.116	0.0776	0.000087	0.00022	0.000034
C	0.0575	0.0349	0.00161	0.001907	0.001359
D	0.105	0.0735	0.000007	0.000015	0.000003
E	0.125	0.0825	0.000256	0.000568	0.000115
F	0.135	0.1076	0.001212	0.001145	0.001284
Sum	0.607	0.4306	0.003735	0.004921	0.003094
Average	0.1012	0.0718			
Covariance			0.000747		
Variance				0.000984	0.000619
Std. Dev (s)				0.031373	0.024874

Illustrations of Calculations

Covariance = Sum of cross products / n − 1 = 0.003735/5 = 0.000747

Var (X) = Sum of squared deviations from the sample mean / n − 1 = 0.004921/5 = 0.000984

Var (Y) = Sum of squared deviations from the sample mean / n − 1 = 0.003094/5 = 0.000619

> **Correlation coefficient** = $r = \dfrac{\text{Cov}(X, Y)}{S_X S_Y} = \dfrac{0.000747}{(0.031373)(0.024874)} = 0.9573$ or 95.73%
>
> The correlation coefficient of 0.9573 suggests that over the period, a strong linear relationship exists between the money supply growth rate and the inflation rate for the countries in the sample.
>
> Note that computed correlation coefficients are only valid if the means and variances of X and Y, as well as the covariance of X and Y, are finite and constant.

Learning objective: Describe the method and three key assumptions of OLS for estimation of parameters.

These assumptions and methods of the OLS are slightly technical but are necessary for the application of probability theory for the calculation of confidence intervals. They are also useful when trying to figure out when OLS analysis will work or is insightful.

Assumption #1—The distribution of the error term has a mean of zero—This means on average we expect there to be no error—that the estimate is a good fit for the population.

Assumption #2—The sample set is independent and identically distributed. Meaning we expect a fair, or random, sample to be taken. We will see this again when talking about heteroskedacity.

Assumption #3—We assume large outliers are going to be unlikely. The OLS method is especially sensitive to outliers and can alter the outcome of a hypothesis test so it is important to graph the data to spot a potential outlier that results from a data entry error. In cases where outliers are known to exist, OLS can give misleading results.

Learning objective: Summarize the benefits of using OLS estimators.

The reading is very brief on this topic. It simply says using OLS is beneficial because everyone else uses it and it is built into almost every data and spreadsheet analysis tool. OLS is also an "unbiased and consistent" estimator meaning the average of the estimate is close to the population and the individual estimates are close to the population (few outliers from assumption 3 above).

All in all, pretty low probability on exam day.

Learning objective: Describe the properties of OLS estimators and their sampling distributions, and explain the properties of consistent estimators in general.

The key property of a consistent estimator is that the average of repeated estimates is close to the actual population. Again this comes back to the "no outliers" assumption, but in financial data sets we know we have fat tails. Understanding why this is important is key to understanding the limitations of OLS. See Examples 3 and 4.

© 2017 Wiley

Learning objective: Interpret the explained sum of squares, the total sum of squares, the residual sum of squares, the standard error of the regression, and the regression R^2.

THE STANDARD ERROR OF ESTIMATE

The standard error of estimate (SEE), also known as the standard error of the regression, is used to measure how well a regression model captures the relationship between the two variables. It indicates how well the regression line "fits" the sample data and is used to determine how certain we can be about a particular prediction of the dependent variable ($\hat{Y}_i$) based on a regression equation. A good way to look at the SEE is that it basically measures the standard deviation of the residual term ($\hat{\varepsilon}_i$) in the regression. At the risk of stating the obvious, the smaller the standard deviation of the residual term (the smaller the standard error of estimate), the more accurate the predictions based on the model. See Example 3.

The formula for the SEE for a linear regression with one independent variable is:

$$SEE = \left(\frac{\sum_{i=1}^{n}(Y_i - \hat{b}_0 - \hat{b}_1 X_i)^2}{n-2} \right)^{1/2} = \left(\frac{\sum_{i=1}^{n}(\hat{\varepsilon}_i)^2}{n-2} \right)^{1/2} = \left(\frac{SSE}{n-2} \right)^{1/2}$$

Note:

- In the numerator of the SEE equation we are essentially calculating the sum of the squared differences between actual and predicted (based on the regression equation) values of the dependent variable.
- We divide the numerator by $n - 2$ (degrees of freedom) to ensure that the estimate of SEE is unbiased.

Example 3: Computing the Standard Error of Estimate

Based on the regression equation: Inflation rate = –0.005 + 0.7591 (Money supply growth rate) compute the standard error of estimate (SEE) for the regression.

Country	Money Supply Growth Rate (X_i)	Inflation Rate (Y_i)	Predicted Inflation Rate ($\hat{Y}_i$)	Regression Residual ($Y_i - \hat{Y}_i$)	Squared Residual ($Y_i - \hat{Y}_i)^2$
A	0.0685	0.0545	0.0470	0.0075	0.000057
B	0.1160	0.0776	0.0830	–0.0054	0.000029
C	0.0575	0.0349	0.0386	–0.0037	0.000014
D	0.1050	0.0735	0.0747	–0.0012	0.000001
E	0.1250	0.0825	0.0899	–0.0074	0.000054
F	0.1350	0.1076	0.0974	0.0102	0.000103
Sum					0.000259

Candidates get VERY confused between SEE and SSE so we have introduced both of them here. SEE is the standard deviation of the error term in the regression while SSE equals the sum of the squared residuals in the regression. SSE (as you will see later in the reading) is used to calculate R^2 and the F-stat for the regression. Also note that the two are related by the following equation: SEE = (SSE/n − 2)$^{0.5}$

Just to illustrate how we obtained the values in this table, let's perform the calculations for Country A:

Predicted inflation rate = −0.005 + 0.7591(0.0685) = 0.046998
Regression residual = 0.0545 − 0.046998 = 0.0075
Squared residual = 0.0075^2 = 0.000057

From the table (by aggregating the values in the last column) we obtain a figure of 0.000259 as the sum of the squared residuals (SSE). This figure is then plugged into the SEE formula to determine the standard error of estimate.

$$SEE = \left(\frac{0.000259}{6-2}\right)^{1/2} = 0.00805 \text{ or } 0.8\%$$

Example 4: Calculating the Coefficient of Determination

From Example 3 we know that the unexplained variation (sum of squared differences between observed and predicted values of the dependent variable) for our regression involving money supply growth rates and inflation rates equals 0.000259 (SSE). Calculate the total variation in inflation rates and then compute the coefficient of determination for the regression.

Solution

The computation of the total variation in the dependent variable (inflation rates) is illustrated in the table below:

Country	Money Supply Growth Rate (X_i)	Inflation Rate (Y_i)	Deviation from Mean $(Y_i - \bar{Y})$	Squared Deviation $(Y_i - \bar{Y})^2$
A	0.0685	0.0545	−0.0173	0.000298
B	0.1160	0.0776	0.0058	0.000034
C	0.0575	0.0349	−0.0369	0.001359
D	0.1050	0.0735	0.0017	0.000003
E	0.1250	0.0825	0.0107	0.000115
F	0.1350	0.1076	0.0358	0.001284
	Average	$(\bar{Y}) = 0.0718$	Sum	0.003094

Just to illustrate how we obtained the values in this table, let's perform the calculations for Country A:

Deviation from mean = 0.0545 − 0.0718 = −0.0173
Squared deviation = −0.0173^3 = 0.000298

> From the table (by aggregating the values in the last column) we obtain a figure of 0.003094 as the sum of the squared deviations of observed values of the dependent variable from their average value. This figure represents the total variation in the dependent variable, and given the unexplained variation in the dependent variable (SSE = 0.000259) can be used to calculate the coefficient of determination for the regression as follows:
>
> $$R^2 = \frac{\text{Total variation} - \text{Unexplained variation}}{\text{Total variation}} = \frac{0.003094 - 0.000259}{0.003094} = 0.9162 \text{ or } 91.62\%$$

THE COEFFICIENT OF DETERMINATION

The coefficient of determination (R^2) tells us how well the independent variable explains the variation in the dependent variable. It measures the fraction of the total variation in the dependent variable that is explained by the independent variable. The coefficient of determination can be calculated in two ways:

1. $R^2 = (r)^2$

    For a linear regression with only one independent variable, the coefficient of determination (R^2) can be calculated by squaring the correlation coefficient (r). In Example 3, we calculated the correlation coefficient between inflation rates and money supply growth from 1990 to 2010 to be 0.9573. Thus, the coefficient of determination for the regression equals 0.9573^2 or 0.9164. What this means is that variation in money supply growth rate explains about 91.64% of the variation in inflation rates across the six countries from 1990 to 2010.

2. The following method can be used to calculate the coefficient of determination for regressions with one or more independent variables.
    - The total variation in the dependent variable (sum of squared deviations of observed values of Y from the average value of Y) denoted by $\sum_{i=1}^{n}(Y_i - \bar{Y})^2$ can be broken down into the variation explained by the independent variable(s) and the variation that remains unexplained by the independent variable(s).
    - The variation in the dependent variable that cannot be explained by the independent variable(s) (sum of squared deviations of actual values of Y from the values predicted by the regression equation) denoted by $\sum_{i=1}^{n}(Y_i - \hat{Y}_i)^2$ is known as unexplained variation.
    - The variation in the dependent variable that cannot be explained by the independent variable(s) (sum of squared deviations of actual values of Y from the values predicted by the regression equation) denoted by $\sum_{i=1}^{n}(\hat{Y}_i - \bar{Y})^2$ is known as explained variation.

The important thing to note is that R^2 measures the percentage of the total variation in the dependent variable that can be explained by the variation in the independent variable. See Example 3.

$$\text{Total variation} = \text{Unexplained variation} + \text{Explained variation}$$

$$R^2 = \frac{\text{Explained variation}}{\text{Total variation}} = \frac{\text{Total variation} - \text{Unexplained variation}}{\text{Total variation}}$$
$$= 1 - \frac{\text{Unexplained variation}}{\text{Total variation}}$$

Learning objective: Interpret the results of an OLS regression.

The interpretation of an OLS regression combines regression analysis with hypothesis testing to evaluate how well our regression is. This is long and complicated and for the FRM exam you won't have to do this start to finish like this, but you do need to know how to do each part because this will definitely be on the exam:

Example 5: Determining the Significance of the Coefficients in a Multiple Regression

Amy is interested in predicting the GMAT scores of students looking to gain admission into MBA programs around the United States. She specifies a regression model with the GMAT score as the dependent variable and the number of hours spent studying for the test and the student's college GPA as the independent variables. The regression is estimated from using data from 50 students and is formulated as:

$$Y_i = b_0 + b_1 X_{1i} + b_2 X_{2i} + \varepsilon_i$$

where:
- Y_i = A student's GMAT score
- b_0 = Intercept term
- X_{1i} = Independent Variable 1: The number of hours a student spends preparing for the test.
- X_{2i} = Independent Variable 2. The student's undergraduate college GPA.

Amy believes that the higher the number of hours spent preparing for the test, the higher the score obtained on the test (i.e., a positive relationship exists between the two variables). Therefore, she sets up her null and alternative hypotheses for testing the significance of the slope coefficient of X_{1i} (the number of hours spent studying) as follows:

$H_0 : b_1 \leq 0$
$H_a : b_1 > 0$

Amy also believes that the higher a student's college GPA, the higher the score obtained on the test (i.e., a positive relationship exists between the two variables). Therefore, she formulates the following hypotheses relating to the slope coefficient of X_{2i} (undergraduate GPA):

$H_0 : b_2 \leq 0$
$H_a : b_2 > 0$

Table 1 shows the results of the regression.

Table 1: Results from Regressing GMAT Scores on Hours of Prep and College GPA

	Coefficient	Standard Error	t-Statistic		
Intercept	231.3476	47.3286	4.8881		
Number of hours of study	1.103	0.0939	11.7465		
College GPA	68.3342	16.5938	4.1181		
ANOVA	df	SS	MS	F	Significance F
Regression	2	444,866.09	222,433.04	73.12	0
Residual	47	142,983.91	3,042.21		
Total	49	587,850			
Standard Error	55.1562				
R Square	0.7568				
Observations	50				
Adjusted R Square	0.7464				

As the first step in multiple regression analysis, an analyst should evaluate the overall significance of the regression. The ANOVA section of the regression results provides us with the data that is used to evaluate the overall explanatory power and significance of the regression. For now, we will move directly into tests relating to the significance of the individual regression coefficients and assume that overall, the regression is significant.

Just like in simple linear regression, the magnitude of the regression coefficients in a multiple regression does not tell us anything about their significance in explaining the variation in the dependent variable. Hypothesis tests must be performed on these coefficients to evaluate their importance in explaining the variation in the dependent variable.

First we evaluate the belief that the higher the number of hours spent studying for the test, the higher the score obtained.

$H_0 : b_1 \leq 0$
$H_a : b_1 > 0$

$$t = \text{stat} = \frac{\hat{b}_1 - b_1}{s_{\hat{b}_1}}$$
$$= (1.103 - 0) / 0.0939 = 11.7465$$

The critical t-value at the 5% level of significance for this one-tailed test with 47 (calculated as $n - (k + 1) = 50 - 3$) degrees of freedom is 1.678.

The t-stat (11.7465) is greater than the critical t-value (1.678). Therefore, at the 5% level of significance, we can reject the null hypothesis and conclude that the higher the number of hours a student spends studying for the GMAT, the higher the score obtained.

> Next, we evaluate the belief that the higher the student's college GPA, the higher the GMAT score obtained
>
> $H_0 : b_2 \leq 0$
> $H_a : b_2 > 0$
>
> $$t = \text{stat} = \frac{\hat{b}_2 - b_2}{s_{\hat{b}_2}} = (68.3342 - 0)/16.5938 = 4.1181$$
>
> The critical t-value at the 5% level of significance for this one-tailed test with 47 degrees of freedom is 1.678.
>
> The t-stat (4.1181) is greater than the critical t-value (1.678). Therefore, at the 5% level of significance we can reject the null hypothesis and conclude that the higher the student's undergraduate GPA, the higher the GMAT score obtained.
>
> Most software programs also report a p-value for each regression coefficient. The p-value represents the lowest level of significance at which a null hypothesis that the population value of the regression coefficient equals 0 can be rejected in a two-tailed test. For example, if the p-value for a regression coefficient equals 0.03, the null hypothesis that the coefficient equals 0 can be rejected at the 5% level of significance, but not at the 2% significance level. The lower the p-value, the stronger the case for rejecting the null hypothesis.

Based on the results of her two-independent variable regression, Amy must be careful not to expect the difference in the expected GMAT scores of two individuals whose total number of hours of prep differed by one hour to be 1.103 points. This is because in all likelihood, the college GPAs of the two individuals would differ as well, which would have an impact on their GMAT scores. Therefore, 1.103 points is the expected net effect of each additional hour spent studying for the test (net of the impact of the student's GPA) on her expected GMAT score.

Interpreting the intercept term of the multiple regression equation is fairly straightforward. It represents the expected value of the dependent variable if all the independent variables in the regression equal 0.

Stock, Chapter 5

James Stock and Mark Watson, *Introduction to Econometrics*, Brief Edition (Boston: Pearson Education, 2008). Chapter 5. Regression with a Single Regressor

After completing this reading you should be able to:

- Calculate, and interpret confidence intervals for regression coefficients.
- Interpret the p-value.
- Interpret hypothesis tests about regression coefficients.
- Evaluate the implications of homoskedasticity and heteroskedasticity.
- Determine the conditions under which the OLS is the best linear conditionally unbiased estimator.
- Explain the Gauss-Markov theorem and its limitations and alternatives to the OLS.
- Apply and interpret the t-statistic when the sample size is small.

Learning objective: Interpret hypothesis tests about regression coefficients.

Learning objective: Calculate, and interpret confidence intervals for regression coefficients.

CONFIDENCE INTERVALS FOR REGRESSION COEFFICIENTS

A confidence interval is a range of values within which we believe the true population parameter (e.g., b_1) lies, with a certain degree of confidence ($1 - \alpha$). Let's work with the same example that we just used to perform the hypothesis test on ABC Stock's beta to illustrate how confidence intervals are computed and interpreted.

$$\hat{b}_j \pm (t_c \times s_{\hat{b}_j})$$

estimated regression coefficient ± (critical t-value)(coefficient standard error)

The critical t-value is a two-tailed value computed based on the significance level (1 – confidence level) and $n - (k + 1)$ degrees of freedom.

Example 1: Confidence Interval for a Regression Coefficient in a Multiple Regression

Calculate the 95% confidence interval for the estimated coefficient of number of hours spent studying in our GMAT score example.

Solution

The critical t-value for a two-tailed test at the 5% level of significance with 47 degrees of freedom is 2.012. Therefore, the confidence interval for the slope coefficient b_1 is:

$1.103 \pm (2.012)(0.0939) = 0.914$ to 1.291

> Since the hypothesized value (0) of the slope coefficient (b_1) of the independent variable, number of hours spent studying (X_1), does not lie within the computed 95% confidence interval, we reject the null hypothesis that the slope coefficient, b_1, equals 0 at the 5% level of significance.

Predicting the Dependent Variable

Predicting the value of the dependent variable from the multiple regression equation given forecasted or assumed values of the independent variables in the regression is quite straightforward. We simply follow the steps listed below:

- Obtain estimates for $\hat{b}_0, \hat{b}_1, \hat{b}_2, ..., \hat{b}_k$ of regression parameters $b_0, b_1, b_2, ..., b_k$.
- Determine the assumed values for independent variables $\hat{X}_1, \hat{X}_2, ..., \hat{X}_k$.
- Compute the value of the dependent variable, $\hat{Y}_i$, using the equation
$$\hat{Y}_i = \hat{b}_0 + \hat{b}_1 \hat{X}_{1i} + \hat{b}_2 \hat{X}_{2i} + ... + ... + \hat{b}_k \hat{X}_{ki}$$

Do keep in mind that all the independent variables in the regression equation (regardless of whether or not their estimated slope coefficients are significantly different from 0), must be used in predicting the value of the dependent variable. See Example 2.

> **Example 2: Predicting the Dependent Variable**
>
> Amy has put in 270 hours of study for her upcoming GMAT test. Her undergraduate college GPA was 3.64. Based on her regression model, what score should she expect to obtain on her test?
>
> **Solution**
>
> GMAT score = 231.35 + 1.103 (no. of hours) + 68.3342 (college GPA)
> $\qquad\qquad$ = 231.35 + 1.103(270) + 68.3342(3.64)
> $\qquad\qquad$ = 777.90 or approximately 778
>
> Amy's regression model predicts a score of approximately 778 for her on the GMAT based on 270 hours of prep and a 3.64 college GPA.

Note that when using the estimated regression equation to make predictions of the dependent variable:

- We should be confident that the assumptions of the regression model are met.
- We should be cautious about predictions based on out-of-sample values of the independent variables (values that are outside the range of data on which the model was estimated) as these predictions can be unreliable.

Learning objective: Interpret the *p*-value.

In hypothesis testing, we compare the test statistic to a critical value and decide to either reject the null hypothesis or not to reject it. For example, if the critical value of z is 2.33 and the computed value of the test statistic is 2.37, the decision is to reject the null hypothesis.

We can easily determine exactly how confident we are in rejecting the null hypothesis *by using a* computer to calculate the ***p*-value**, which is *the probability of observing a value of the test statistic at least as extreme as the value actually observed, assuming that the null hypothesis is true.*

To test a hypothesis, we can compare the *p*-value with the significance level. *If the p-value is smaller than the significance level, then the null hypothesis is rejected. Otherwise, it is not rejected.*

Example 3

Suppose the test statistic is equal to 3.30, the significance level is 0.05, and the test is a two-tailed *z*-test. Will the null hypothesis be rejected? What is the *p*-value?

Solution

At a significance level of 0.05 and with a two-tailed test, the critical values will be −1.96 and +1.96; therefore, the null hypothesis will be rejected, and the alternative hypothesis will be accepted. The determination of the *p*-value requires that we look up 3.30 in our probability tables. We find that the probability that an observed *z*-value is less than or equal to 3.30 is 0.9995; therefore, the probability that we find one that extreme is 1 − 0.9995 = 0.0005. The *p*-value is thus 0.0005.

In addition to testing the hypothesis, the *p*-value gives information on the strength of our decision. A very small *p*-value, say 0.001, means there is a very small chance that H_0 is true. On the other hand, a *p*-value of .40 means that H_0 is not rejected, and we also have some evidence that it is *not false*.

Here is a guide to help interpret *p*-values:

If the *p*-value is less than .10, we have *some* evidence that H_0 is not true.
If the *p*-value is less than .05, we have *strong* evidence that H_0 is not true.
If the *p*-value is less than .01, we have *very strong* evidence that H_0 is not true.
If the *p*-value is less than .001, we have *extremely strong* evidence that H_0 is not true.

p-VALUES AND SIGNIFICANCE LEVELS

You will notice that a *p*-value is essentially a significance level. Note that as significance levels get smaller, it becomes harder to reject the null hypothesis. For very small significance levels, the burden to disprove the null hypothesis is quite heavy. Of course, significance levels are set prior to computing the test statistic.

The *p*-value tells you something about the rarity of the test statistic value, after it is observed. A very small *p*-value implies that a very rare event has been observed, one that may well meet the heavy burden of proof required to reject the null hypothesis. This is how *p*-values and significance levels are related—they are the same concept, but one is specified prior to observing data and sets a hurdle, while the other describes the relative rarity of the data once it has been observed.

Recall before that I said the critical *t* is often written as t_a? Well, the alpha portion determines the percentage of area that is left in the tail. For example, a 95% level of significance would be an alpha of 5%. This idea of level of significance is closely related to the *p*-value. Up until this point, we have chosen round numbers as our level of significance, such as 95% or 99%, but in reality we can get much more information if we **choose the lowest level of significance where we can reject the null hypothesis.** The *p*-value then may be higher or lower than an arbitrary 95% or 99% level of significance. Whether or not a *p*-value is statistically significant is not determined by a test as with the critical *t*, but whether we are willing to accept the risk of a type I error that is implied by the *p*-value. Stated differently, the ***p*-value is the risk of making a type I error.**

Learning objective: Evaluate the implications of homoskedasticity and heteroskedasticity.

A homoskedastic regression might look like Figure 1.

Figure 1. A Homoskedastic Regression

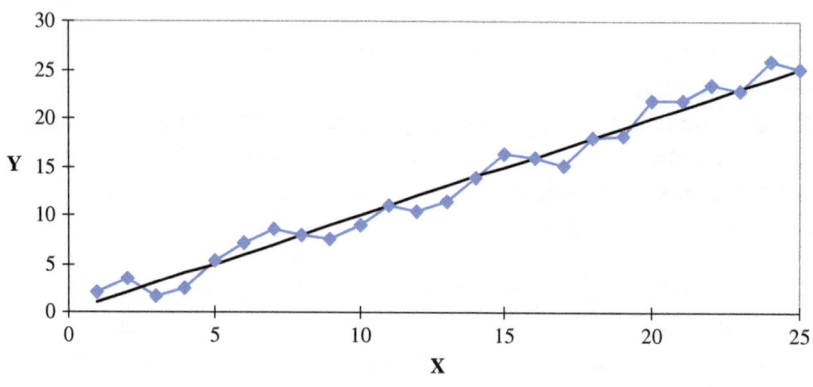

If, on the other hand, the variance of error terms is not constant across all observations, we have a **heteroskedastic regression**. An example of a heteroskedastic regression would look like Figure 2:

Figure 2. A Heteroskedastic Regression

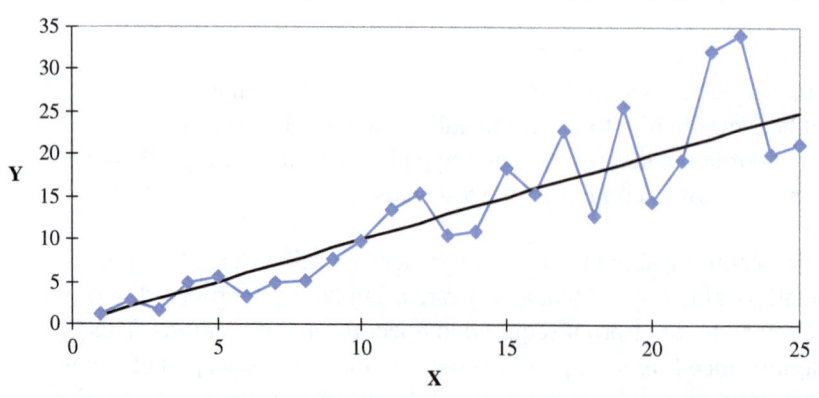

Here it is fairly obvious that the variance error is increasing with the larger values of X.

Recall assumption four of multiple regression: *Error terms have the same variance across all observations*. This is referred to as **homoskedasticity**.

There are two major types of heteroskedasticity. **Unconditional heteroskedasticity** *occurs when the heteroskedasticity is not correlated with the independent variables of the regression equation*. Unconditional heteroskedasticity may technically violate assumption four of the regression model; however, it does not often lead to significant errors in statistical inference.

The other kind of heteroskedasticity is **conditional heteroskedasticity**. This is (unfortunately) the more common type, and it refers to the fact that *the variance in the error term is correlated with the values of the independent variables in the regression*. This is the type of heteroskedasticity that appears in Figure 2, for the variance appears to be associated with the value of X (the larger X is, the larger the variance in the error term is). It is possible, however, to detect and correct for conditional heteroskedasticity; some software packages have this feature.

Again, same as in the simple case.

CONSEQUENCES OF HETEROSKEDASTICITY

Typically, heteroskedasticity results in standard errors that are too small, and thus t-statistics that are too large. Consequently, relationships that appear significant in the regression results may not be significant at all.

Learning objective: Explain the Gauss-Markov theorem and its limitations, and alternatives to the OLS.

Learning objective: Determine the conditions under which the OLS is the best linear conditionally unbiased estimator.

The Gauss-Markov assumptions are beyond the scope of the FRM exam but just know the Gauss-Markov theorem is that if all these special assumptions are true, then the OLS estimator for the slope in a regression is BLUE or Best Linear Unbiased Estimator.

Often in finance we have errors that are heteroskedastic, which violates the OLS assumptions and makes OLS no longer the best estimate.

A way to fix this is called the weighted least squares estimator but is almost never used in practice. It basically transforms the error terms into homoskedastic and therefore this weighting method becomes BLUE.

In the case of known extreme outliers, which we know OLS is sensitive to, we can use the Least Absolute Deviations Estimator method that utilizes the absolute value of errors instead of squared errors.

Learning objective: Apply and interpret the t-statistic when the sample size is small.

If the sample size is small but we know that three certain things are true about the distribution, we can be certain the student t-distribution can be used.

Those three things are collectively called the homoskedastic normal regression assumptions and they are:

1. The three assumptions of OLS: error term has mean zero, sample is i.i.d, and large outliers are unlikely.
2. Error terms are homoskedastic.
3. Error terms are normally distributed.

There are only a few lists you need to know for the exam where they explicitly ask about the list and I think this is one of them.

Stock, Chapter 6

James Stock and Mark Watson, *Introduction to Econometrics,* Brief Edition (Boston: Pearson Education, 2008). Chapter 6. Linear Regression with Multiple Regressors

After completing this reading you should be able to:

- Define and interpret omitted variable bias, and describe the methods for addressing this bias.
- Distinguish between single and multiple regression.
- Interpret the slope coefficient in a multiple regression.
- Describe homoskedasticity and heteroskedasticity in a multiple regression.
- Describe the OLS estimator in a multiple regression.
- Calculate and interpret measures of fit in multiple regression.
- Explain the assumptions of the multiple linear regression model.
- Explain the concept of imperfect and perfect multicollinearity and their implications.

Learning objective: Define and interpret omitted variable bias, and describe the methods for addressing this bias.

In multiple regression there exists the possibility that a variable which is actually correlated with the regressor is omitted from analysis. In this case, the OLS will have what is called omitted variable bias. The reverse of this concept is getting an improved R squared value in a regression analysis when we add more and more variables and thereby generate spurious correlation.

The key way to address variable bias is to slice the data into groups and then perform multiple regression analysis on the sample. I believe omitted variable bias is just a setup for multiple regression and won't likely be on the exam. This reading is important, just not this learning objective.

$$Y_t = b_0 + = b_1 X_1 + b_2 X_{2t} + b_k X_{kt} + \varepsilon_n$$

Where:

$t = 1, 2, ..., t$ observations

$Y_t = t$th observation of the dependent variable

Learning objective: Distinguish between single and multiple regression.

In regression analysis, we are often interested in whether the dependent variable is related to more than one independent variable. For example, we may wish to study the returns of a small capitalization mutual fund and see how they may relate to the returns of the small-cap value sector and the small-cap growth sector. To do this, we can use a **multiple linear regression** model:

$X_j = j$th independent variable

$X_{jt} = t$th observation of the jth independent variable

$b_0 =$ intercept of the regression equation

$b_k =$ coefficient (slope) of the kth independent variable

$\varepsilon_t =$ error at the tth observation

In the equation above, b_1 is the coefficient, or slope, associated with the 1st independent variable. It tells you how much Y_t, the dependent variable, changes per 1 unit change in the independent variable X_1. So suppose that, in a given observation period, none of the independent variables (the X_j) change except for X_1, which changes from 12 to 13. If the slope is 2, then the dependent variable Y_t will increase by 2 just for the one unit increase in X_1.

An example of a multiple linear regression is shown below where we have the multiple explanatory random variables K_1 and K_2 describing the outcome of the random variable Y. The J term in this case represents the slope intercept and is additional to explanatory variables that seek to explain the behavior in the dependent variable Y.

$$E(Y|X_n) = J_1 + K_1X_1 + K_2X_2 + \varepsilon_n$$

A two-variable linear regression is also called a simple linear regression since there is one independent variable describing one dependent variable. Since we have two variables refer to the two variable linear regression or a simple linear regression.

Learning objective: Describe homoskedasticity and heteroskedasticity in a multiple regression.

Heteroskedasticity occurs when the variance of the error term in the regression is not constant across observations. Figure 1 shows the scatter plot and regression line for a model with homoskedastic errors. There seems to be no systematic relationship between the regression residuals (vertical distances between the data points and the regression line) and the independent variable. Figure 2 shows the scatter plot and regression line for a model with heteroskedastic errors. Notice that the regression residuals appear to increase in size as the value of the independent variable increases.

Figure 1: Regression with Homoskedasticity

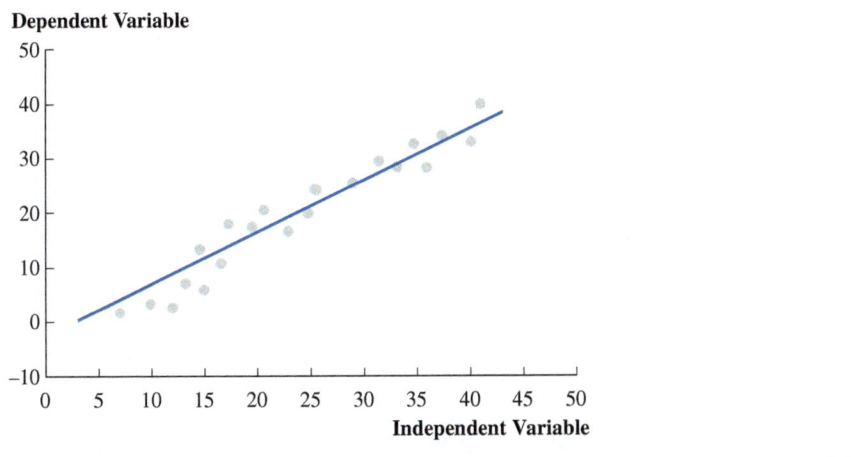

Figure 2: Regression with Heteroskedasticity

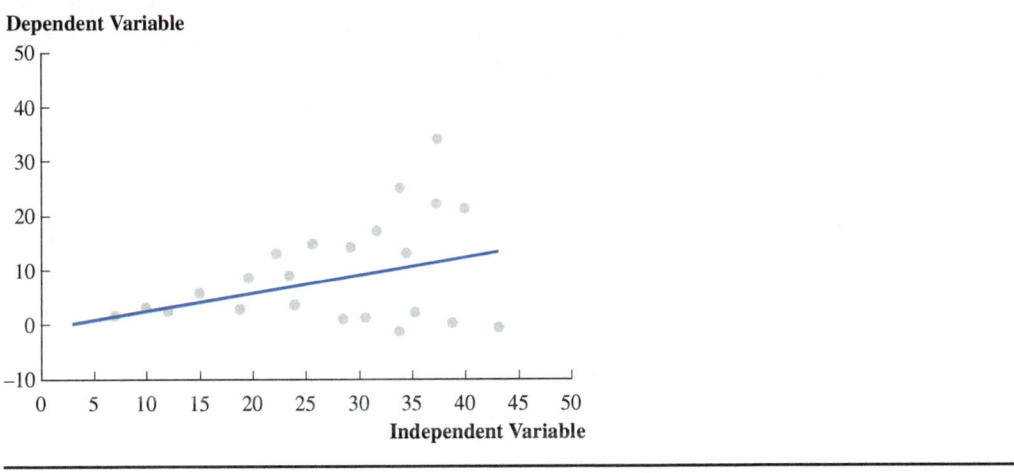

EFFECTS OF HETEROSKEDASTICITY

Heteroskedasticity does not affect the consistency of estimators of regression parameters. However, it can lead to mistakes in inferences made from parameter estimates.

The *F*-test for the overall significance of the regression becomes unreliable as the MSE becomes a biased estimator of the true population variance.

The *t*-tests for the significance of each regression coefficient become unreliable as the estimates of the standard errors of regression coefficients become biased.

Typically, in regressions with financial data, standard errors of regression coefficients are underestimated and *t*-stats are inflated due to heteroskedasticity. Therefore, ignoring heteroskedasticity results in significant relationships being found when none actually exist. (Null hypotheses are rejected too often.)

TWO TYPES OF HETEROSKEDASTICITY
- Unconditional heteroskedasticity occurs when the heteroskedasticity of the variance in the error term is not related to the independent variables in the regression. Unconditional heteroskedasticity does not create major problems for regression analysis.
- Conditional heteroskedasticity occurs when the heteroskedasticity in the error variance is correlated with the independent variables in the regression. While conditional heteroskedasticity does create problems for statistical inference, it can be easily identified and corrected.

Learning objective: Interpret the slope coefficient in a multiple regression.

Learning objective: Describe the OLS estimator in a multiple regression.

The existence of an error term within a regression implies that we are not dealing with a complete population but rather a sample. By definition, the characteristics of a sample will change from sample to sample. We know this from a previous learning objective. To take this further, we know things that we are estimating are called random variables and we can use sampling theory to make a whole host of characterizations about the behavior of the random variables and by extension, the regression itself.

The standard error is another phrase for the square of the variance of the random variables that describe key aspects of the regression (the coefficients). Therefore, the standard error, SE, is just like standard deviation in that it is the "standardized" variance but in this case it describes the parameters (estimates) in an ordinary least squared regression model.

These are only estimations of the true slope and intercept since we don't have total information about the population. Remember the existence of an error term means we are dealing with a sample. If you see this on the exam, I think they will ask you to calculate the variance of the slope term in the regression and ignore the variance of the intercept, which is arguably less important.

The formula you should know is:

$$Var(Slope) = \frac{\sigma^2}{\sum (x - \bar{x})^2}$$

where sigma in the numerator is the error variance (this will be given to you on the exam) and the denominator shows the sample minus the average sample squared. We have seen this before. While this is the actual formula, I think it is useless on exam day since they would have to give you a huge table of data to calculate either. Consequently, I think this is a low probability for the exam. One exception would be that they could give you the "total sum of squares" value, which would describe the denominator and then give you the variance of the error term. In this case, you could plug in the values but would need to know that the total sum of squares (often referred to as SST in text books) goes in the denominator and the variance of the error term goes in the numerator.

As with any interpretation based on variance, the lower the variance, the greater the explanatory value with a higher degree of certainty.

Learning objective: Calculate and interpret measures of fit in multiple regression.

To answer the question "How well do the independent variables as a group explain the variation in the dependent variable?" in our multiple regression, we perform an F-test with a null hypothesis that all the slope coefficients in the regression simultaneously equal zero versus an alternative hypothesis that at least one of the slope coefficients in the regression does not equal zero.

$$H_0 : b_1 = b_2 = ... = b_k = 0$$
$$H_a : \text{At least one of the slope coefficients} \neq 0$$

If none of the independent variables significantly explain the variation in the dependent variable, none of the slope coefficients should be significantly different from zero. However, in a multiple regression, we cannot test the hypothesis that all the slope coefficients equal zero based on t-tests on the individual slope coefficients. This is because the individual t-tests do not account for the effects of the correlation or interaction between the independent variables. The F-test and individual t-tests on the slope coefficients may offer conflicting conclusions in the following scenarios:

1. We may be able to reject the null hypothesis that all the slope coefficients equal zero based on the F-test (and conclude that the regression model significantly explains the variation in the dependent variable) even though none of the individual slope coefficients appear significant based on the individual t-tests. (This is a classic symptom of multicollinearity, which we discuss in detail later in the reading).
2. We may fail to reject the null hypothesis that all the slope coefficients equal zero based on the F-test (and conclude that the regression model does not significantly explain the variation in the dependent variable) even though the individual slope coefficients appear to be statistically different from zero based on the individual t-tests.

To calculate the F-stat (test statistic when testing the hypothesis that all the slope coefficients in a multiple regression are jointly equal to zero) we need the following inputs, which are typically included in the ANOVA section of the regression results.

- Total number of observations, n.
- Total number of regression coefficients that must be estimated $(k + 1)$ where k equals the number of slope coefficients.
- The sum of squared errors or residuals (SSE) which represents unexplained variation.

$$\sum_{i=1}^{n}(Y_i - \hat{Y}_i)^2 = \sum_{i=1}^{n}\hat{\varepsilon}_i^2$$

- The regression sum of squares (RSS) which represents explained variation.

$$\sum_{i=1}^{n}(\hat{Y}_i - \bar{Y})^2$$

The *F*-stat measures how well the regression model explains the variation in the dependent variable. The greater the *F*-stat, the better the performance of the regression model in explaining the variation in the dependent variable. The *F*-stat measures the ratio of the mean regression sum of squares (MSR) to the mean squared error (MSE). It is calculated a follows:

$$F\text{-stat} = \frac{MSR}{MSE} = \frac{RSS/k}{SSE/[n-(k+1)]}$$

Note that the *F*-test is a one-tailed test (even though the null hypothesis contains the "=" sign) with the critical *F*-value computed at the desired level of significance with k and $n - (k + 1)$ degrees of freedom for the numerator and denominator respectively. See Example 1.

> **Example 1: Testing Whether All the Population Regression Coefficients Equal Zero**
>
> Evaluate the significance of Amy's two-independent variable regression in explaining students' GMAT scores at the 5% level of significance. An excerpt from the regression results is reproduced in Table 1:
>
> **Table 1: Excerpt**
>
> | ANOVA | df | SS | MS | F | Significance F |
> |---|---|---|---|---|---|
> | Regression | 2 | 444,866.09 | 222,433.04 | 73.12 | 0.00 |
> | Residual | 47 | 142,983.91 | 3,042.21 | | |
> | Total | 49 | 587.850 | | | |
>
> **Solution**
>
> $H_0 : b_1 = b_2 = 0$
>
> H_a : At least one of the slope coefficients $\neq 0$
>
> $$F\text{-stat} = \frac{444,866.09/2}{142,983.91/47} = 73.12$$
>
> At the 5% significance level, the critical *F*-value with 2 and 47 degrees of freedom for the numerator and denominator respectively is between 3.15 and 3.23.
>
> Since the *F*-stat (73.12) is greater than the critical *F*-value, we reject the null hypothesis that the slope coefficients on both the independent variables equal zero. We conclude that at least one of the slope coefficients in the regression is significantly different from 0, which basically implies that at least one of the independent variables in the regression explains the variation in the dependent variable to a significant extent. The *p*-value of the *F*-stat (0) means that the smallest level of significance at which the null hypothesis can be rejected is practically 0. The *p*-value also (as we might expect) suggests that there is a strong case for rejecting the null hypothesis.

Learning objective: Explain the assumptions of the multiple linear regression model.

Assumptions of the Multiple Linear Regression Model

The classical normal multiple linear regression model makes the following six assumptions:

- The relationship between the dependent variable (Y) and the independent variables ($X_1, X_2, ..., X_k$) is linear.
- The independent variables ($X_1, X_2, ..., X_k$) are not random and no exact linear relationship exists between two or more independent variables.
- The expected value of the error term, conditioned on the independent variables, is zero: $E(\varepsilon| X_1, X_2, ..., X_k) = 0$.
- The variance of the error term is the same for all observations. $E(\varepsilon_i^2) = \sigma_e^2$.
- The error term is uncorrelated across observations. $E(\varepsilon_i \varepsilon_j) = 0, j \neq i$.
- The error term is normally distributed.

Learning objective: Explain the concept of imperfect and perfect multicollinearity and their implications.

MULTICOLLINEARITY

Multicollinearity occurs when two or more independent variables (or combinations of independent variables) in a regression are highly correlated with each other. Perfect multicollinearity is where one of the regressors is a perfect linear function of the other regressors, making it impossible to compute the OLS estimator.

EFFECTS OF MULTICOLLINEARITY

- Multicollinearity does not affect the consistency of OLS estimates and regression coefficients, but makes them inaccurate and unreliable.
- It becomes difficult to isolate the impact of each independent variable on the dependent variable.
- The standard errors for the regression coefficients are inflated, which results in t-stats becoming too small and less powerful (in terms of their ability to reject null hypotheses).

Stock, Chapter 7

James Stock and Mark Watson, *Introduction to Econometrics,* Brief Edition (Boston: Pearson Education, 2008). Chapter 7. Hypothesis Tests and Confidence Intervals in Multiple Regression

After completing this reading you should be able to:

- Construct, apply, and interpret hypothesis tests and confidence intervals for a single coefficient in a multiple regression.
- Construct, apply, and interpret hypothesis tests and confidence intervals for multiple coefficients in a multiple regression.
- Interpret the *F*-statistic.
- Interpret tests of single restrictions involving multiple coefficients.
- Interpret confidence sets for multiple coefficients.
- Identify examples of omitted variable bias in multiple regressions.
- Interpret the R^2 and adjusted-R^2 in a multiple regression.

Learning objective: Construct, apply, and interpret hypothesis tests and confidence intervals for a single coefficient in a multiple regression.

Learning objective: Construct, apply, and interpret hypothesis tests and confidence intervals for multiple coefficients in a multiple regression.

	Coefficient	Standard Error	*t*-Statistic		
Intercept	231.3476	47.3286	4.8881		
Number or hours of study	1.103	0.0939	11.7465		
College GPA	68.3342	16.5938	4.1181		
ANOVA	**df**	**SS**	**MS**	**F**	**Significance F**
Regression	2	444,866.09	222,433.04	73.12	0
Residual	47	142,983.91	3,042.21		
Total	49	587,850			
Standard Error	55.1562				
R Square	0.7568				
Observations	50				
Adjusted R Square	0.7464				

CONFIDENCE INTERVALS

A confidence interval for a regression coefficient in a multiple regression is constructed in the same manner as we demonstrated in the previous reading, when we constructed a confidence interval for a regression coefficient in a simple linear regression. The confidence interval is constructed as follows:

$$\hat{b}_j \pm (t_c \times s_{\hat{b}_j})$$

estimated regression coefficient $\pm$ (critical t-value)(coefficient standard error)

The critical t-value is a two-tailed value computed based on the significance level (1 − confidence level) and $n − (k + 1)$ degrees of freedom.

Example 1

Calculate the 95% confidence interval for the estimated coefficient of number of hours spent studying in our GMAT score example.

Solution

The critical t-value for a two-tailed test at the 5% level of significance with 47 degrees of freedom is 2.012. Therefore, the confidence interval for the slope coefficient b_1 is:

$$1.103 \pm (2.012)(0.0939) = 0.914 \text{ to } 1.291$$

Since the hypothesized value (0) of the slope coefficient (b_1) of the independent variable, number of hours spent studying (X_1), does not lie within the computed 95% confidence interval, we reject the null hypothesis that the slope coefficient, b_1, equals 0 at the 5% level of significance.

Predicting the value of the dependent variable from the multiple regression equation given forecasted or assumed values of the independent variables in the regression is quite straightforward. We simply follow the steps listed below:

- Obtain estimates for $\hat{b}_0, \hat{b}_1, \hat{b}_2, ..., \hat{b}_k$ of regression parameters $b_0, b_1, b_2, ..., b_k$.
- Determine the assumed values for independent variables $\hat{X}_1, \hat{X}_2, ..., \hat{X}_k$.
- Compute the value of the dependent variable, $\hat{Y}_1$, using the equation

$$\hat{Y}_i = \hat{b}_0 + \hat{b}_1 \hat{X}_{1i} + \hat{b}_2 \hat{X}_{2i} + ... + \hat{b}_k \hat{X}_{ki}$$

Do keep in mind that all the independent variables in the regression equation (regardless of whether or not their estimated slope coefficients are significantly different from 0), must be used in predicting the value of the dependent variable. See Example 2.

> **Example 2**
>
> Amy has put in 270 hours of study for her upcoming GMAT test. Her undergraduate college GPA was 3.64. Based on her regression model, what score should she expect to obtain on her test?
>
> **Solution**
>
> GMAT score = 231.35 + 1.103(no. of hours) + 68.3342(college GPA)
> = 231.35 + 1.103(270) + 68.3342(3.64)
> = 777.90 or approximately 778
>
> Amy's regression model predicts a score of approximately 778 for her on the GMAT based on 270 hours of prep and a 3.64 college GPA.

Note that when using the estimated regression equation to make predictions of the dependent variable:

- We should be confident that the assumptions of the regression model are met.
- We should be cautious about predictions based on out-of-sample values of the independent variables (values that are outside the range of data on which the model was estimated) as these predictions can be unreliable.

Learning objective: Interpret the *F*-statistic.

TESTING WHETHER ALL THE POPULATION REGRESSION COEFFICIENTS EQUAL ZERO

In Example 1, we illustrated how to conduct hypothesis tests on the individual regression coefficients. We deferred the discussion relating to evaluation of the significance of the estimated regression model as a whole. To address the question, "How well do the independent variables as a group explain the variation in the dependent variable?," we perform an *F*-test with a null hypothesis that all the slope coefficients in the regression simultaneously equal zero versus an alternative hypothesis that at least one of the slope coefficients in the regression does not equal zero.

> $H_0: b_1 = b_2 = ... = b_k = 0$
>
> H_a: At least one of the slope coefficients $\neq 0$

If none of the independent variables significantly explain the variation in the dependent variable, none of the slope coefficients should be significantly different from zero. However, in a multiple regression, we cannot test the hypothesis that all the slope coefficients equal zero based on *t*-tests on the individual slope coefficients. This is because the individual *t*-tests do not account for the effects of the correlation or interaction between the independent variables. The *F*-test and individual *t*-tests on the slope coefficients may offer conflicting conclusions in the following scenarios:

$$\sum_{i=1}^{n}(\hat{Y}_i - \bar{Y})$$

1. We may be able to reject the null hypothesis that all the slope coefficients equal zero based on the *F*-test (and conclude that the regression model significantly explains the variation in the dependent variable), even though none of the individual slope coefficients appear significant based on the individual *t*-tests.
2. We may fail to reject the null hypothesis that all the slope coefficients equal zero based on the *F*-test (and conclude that the regression model does not significantly explain the variation in the dependent variable) even though the individual slope coefficients appear to be statistically different from zero based on the individual *t*-tests.

To calculate the *F*-stat (test statistic when testing the hypothesis that all the slope coefficients in a multiple regression are jointly equal to zero) we need the following inputs, which are typically included in the ANOVA section of the regression results.

- Total number of observations, *n*.
- Total number of regression coefficients that must be estimated (*k* + 1), where *k* equals the number of slope coefficients.
- The sum of squared errors or residuals (SSE) which represents unexplained variation.
- The regression sum of squares (RSS) which represents explained variation.

$$\sum_{i=1}^{n}(Y_i - \hat{Y}_i)^2 = \sum_{i=1}^{n}\hat{\varepsilon}_i^2$$

The *F*-stat measures how well the regression model explains the variation in the dependent variable. The greater the *F*-stat, the better the performance of the regression model in explaining the variation in the dependent variable. The *F*-stat measures the ratio of the mean regression sum of squares (MSR) to the mean squared error (MSE). It is calculated as follows:

$$F\text{-stat} = \frac{MSR}{MSE} = \frac{RSS/k}{SSE/[n-(k+1)]}$$

Note that the *F*-test is a one-tailed test (even though the null hypothesis contains the "=" sign) with the critical *F*-value computed at the desired level of significance with *k* and *n* − (*k* + 1) degrees of freedom for the numerator and denominator respectively. See Example 3.

> **Example 3: Testing Whether All the Population Regression Coefficients Equal Zero**
>
> Evaluate the significance of Amy's two-independent variable regression in explaining students' GMAT scores at the 5% level of significance. An excerpt from the regression results is reproduced in Table 1:
>
> **Table 1: Excerpt**
>
> | ANOVA | df | SS | MS | F | Significance F |
> |---|---|---|---|---|---|
> | Regression | 2 | 444,866.09 | 222,433.04 | 73.12 | 0.00 |
> | Residual | 47 | 142,983.91 | 3,042.21 | | |
> | Total | 49 | 587,850 | | | |
>
> **Solution**
>
> $H_0: b_1 = b_2 = 0$
> $H_a:$ At least one of the slope coefficients $\neq 0$
>
> $$F\text{-stat} = \frac{444{,}866.09/2}{142{,}983.91/47} = 73.12$$
>
> At the 5% significance level, the critical F-value with 2 and 47 degrees of freedom for the numerator and denominator respectively is between 3.15 and 3.23.
>
> Since the F-stat (73.12) is greater than the critical F-value, we reject the null hypothesis that the slope coefficients on both the independent variables equal zero. We conclude that at least one of the slope coefficients in the regression is significantly different from 0, which basically implies that at least one of the independent variables in the regression explains the variation in the dependent variable to a significant extent. The p-value of the F-stat (0) means that the smallest level of significance at which the null hypothesis can be rejected is practically 0. The p-value also (as we might expect) suggests that there is a strong case for rejecting the null hypothesis.

At the 5% significance level, the critical F-value with 2 and 47 degrees of freedom for the numerator and denominator respectively is between 3.15 and 3.23. Since the F-stat (73.12) is greater than the critical F-value, we reject the null hypothesis that the slope coefficients on both the independent variables equal zero. We conclude that at least one of the slope coefficients in the regression is significantly different from 0, which basically implies that at least one of the independent variables in the regression explains the variation in the dependent variable to a significant extent. The p-value of the F-stat (0) means that the smallest level of significance at which the null hypothesis can be rejected is practically 0. The p-value also (as we might expect) suggests that there is a strong case for rejecting the null hypothesis.

Learning objective: Interpret tests of single restrictions involving multiple coefficients.

When this learning objective refers to "tests" it means the t-test in our hypothesis testing. A single restriction in a multiple coefficient regression means we are holding one value the same and changing another variable—akin to partial derivatives in calculus. The interpretation of this restriction is just the same as before but we have a different t-statistic to test because we changed the null hypothesis when we changed the other variable.

It is easy to get bogged down in the math in this reading, but focus on what GARP is asking: interpret the test and the interpretation is just the same as before, just with a different t-statistic.

Learning objective: Identify examples of omitted variable bias in multiple regressions.

Omitted variable bias occurs when one or more regressors are correlated with an omitted variable. In other words our OLS is partially dependent upon a regressor not included in the analysis. We know from R^2 the addition of regressors may increase a regression's predictive power by spurious correlation. So adding variables can create a problem but having too few variables can also be a problem.

This learning objective asks for examples of omitted bias, which is basically everything in finance. Economic models take a few variables and try and predict the entire economy, but we know there are other variables that could impact our regression that aren't included in the model for whatever reason.

The resolution for this, according to the reading, is judgment and expertise in deciding what to include in a multiple regression analysis.

Learning objective: Interpret the R^2 and adjusted-R^2 in a multiple regression.

Recall that the coefficient of determination (R^2) measures how much of the variation in the dependent variable is captured by the independent variables in the regression collectively. It is calculated as:

$$R^2 = \frac{\text{Total variation} - \text{Unexplained variation}}{\text{Total variation}} = \frac{\text{SST} - \text{SSE}}{\text{SST}} = \frac{\text{RSS}}{\text{SST}}$$

In multiple regression analysis, as more and more independent variables are added to the mix, the total amount of unexplained variation will decrease (as the amount of explained variation increases) and the R^2 measure will reflect an improvement on the previous model in terms of the variation explained by the group of independent variables as a proportion of total variation in the dependent variable. This will be the case as long as each newly added independent variable is even slightly correlated with the dependent variable and is not a linear combination of the other independent variables already in the regression model.

Therefore, when evaluating a multiple regression model, analysts typically use adjusted R^2. Adjusted R^2 does not automatically increase when another variable is added to the regression as it is adjusted for degrees of freedom.

It is calculated as:

$$\text{Adjusted } R^2 = \bar{R}^2 = 1 - \left(\frac{n-1}{n-k-1}\right)(1-R^2)$$

Note:

- If $k = 1$, R^2 will be greater than adjusted R^2.
- Adjusted R^2 will decrease if the inclusion of another independent variable in the regression model results in a nominal increase in explained variation (RSS) and R^2.
- Adjusted R^2 can be negative (in which case we consider its value to equal 0) while R^2 can never be negative.
- If we use adjusted R^2 to compare two regression models, we must ensure that the dependent variable is defined in the same manner in the two models and that the sample sizes used to estimate the models are the same.

Example 4: R^2 versus Adjusted R^2

Amy now decides to add a third independent variable (X^{3i}) to her regression model. Upon adding the variable "number of practice tests taken" to the regression, the regression sum of squares (RSS) in the ANOVA increases to 487,342.64, while the sum of squared errors (SSE) falls to 100,507.36.

Calculate the R^2 and adjusted R^2 for the new (three-independent variable) regression model and comment on the values.

Solution

The R^2 and adjusted R^2 for the two-independent variable regression are provided in the table in Example 3.

R^2 = 0.7568 or 75.68%

Adjusted R^2 = 0.7464 or 74.64%

For the new (three-independent variable) regression, R^2 and adjusted R^2 are calculated as:

R^2 = RSS/SST = 487,342.64/587,850 = 0.8290 or 82.90%

The R^2 of the three-independent variable regression is higher (82.9% versus 75.68% earlier), but more important, the adjusted R^2 of the three-independent variable regression is also higher (81.79% versus 74.64% earlier), which suggests that the new model should be preferred. The addition of the third independent variable has improved the model.

$$\text{Adjusted } R^2 = 1 - \left(\frac{n-1}{n-k-1}\right)(1-R^2) = 0.8179 \text{ or } 81.79\%$$

© 2017 Wiley

Diebold, Chapter 5

Francis X. Diebold, *Elements of Forecasting*, 4th Edition (Mason, Ohio: Cengage Learning, 2006). Chapter 5. Modeling and Forecasting Trend

After completing this reading you should be able to:

- Describe linear and nonlinear trends.
- Describe trend models to estimate and forecast trends.
- Compare and evaluate model selection criteria, including mean squared error (MSE), s^2, the Akaike information criterion (AIC), and the Schwarz information criterion (SIC).
- Explain the necessary conditions for a model selection criterion to demonstrate consistency.

Learning objective: Describe linear and nonlinear trends.

A linear trend is one that obviously looks like a line when charted, but it should be thought of as something more like this:

$$T_t = \beta_0 + \beta_1 \, \text{TIME}_t$$

where β_0 is some intercept and we have some regression coefficient as a product of time with some noise around the trend.

These linear trends are far better behaved and predictable but finance is often a non-linear world with trends that exhibit curvature. You can think of these as quadratic trends. The curvature doesn't have to be a perfect fit; there is always noise.

A nonlinear trend may take this type of expression:

$$T_t = \beta_0 + \beta_1 \, \text{TIME}_t + \beta_2 \, \text{TIME}_t^2$$

Learning objective: Describe trend models to estimate and forecast trends.

We have a bit of new notation here from multiple regression so let's step through it. First of all, this is the ordinary least square regression we know as before but the notation looks a lot different.

Remember, we are also going to raise our estimator to the second power because we want to retain the information about the magnitude of deviation, both positive and negative, from the trend line. The way you have to change your thinking here is you are feeding a computer data and forcing a regression instead of performing an ordinary least squared regression yourself.

Our least squared regression now looks like this when we are using trend model:

$$\hat{\theta} = \underset{\theta}{\operatorname{argmin}} \sum_{t=1}^{T} (y_t - T_t(\theta))^2$$

So don't freak out, this is just new notation. Omega in this case is the set of parameters to be estimated. Theta "hat" (on the left) is the forecast of the parameters. As always, subscript t means at that slice of time. y is our series of data. "argmin" is a computer command that finds the smallest value of omega that will minimize the sum of the least squares—that's why we have the term on the right raised to a power of 2.

So let's extend this notation to the most basic linear relationship where we will have two estimates: an intercept and a beta just like this:

$$T_t = \beta_0 + \beta_1 \, \text{TIME}_t$$

Using our new least squared notation, we are going to have a forecast (forecasts always have the "hats" over the variable) and remember y is just the value at that time series.

$$(\hat{\beta}_0, \hat{\beta}_1) = \underset{\beta_0, \beta_1}{\operatorname{argmin}} \sum_{t=1}^{T} (y_t - \beta_0 - \beta_1 \, \text{TIME}_t)^2$$

So now we have an estimated intercept and estimated beta on the left where we minimize the squared differences on the right. Notice the exponent is on the outside of the parenthesis. This is the least squared bit. If we had a nonlinear trend we wanted to fit, it would look like this:

$$(\hat{\beta}_0, \hat{\beta}_1, \hat{\beta}_2) = \underset{\beta_0, \beta_1, \beta_2}{\operatorname{argmin}} \sum_{t=1}^{T} (y_t - \beta_0 - \beta_1 \, \text{TIME}_t - \beta_2 \, \text{TIME}_t^2)^2$$

So we have our intercept, linear slope, and nonlinear (raised to the power of 2) all inside the parentheses raised to the power of 2.

For the exam, do not memorize any of these equations. Do recognize that we are changing the relationship where we are feeding a computer some time series of data, a set of factors, and then it returns an equation that minimizes the difference among all of them whether there is a linear, nonlinear, or combination of both.

So far, we have only established a way to fit trend models to data sets without concern for causality or predictive power. Next we want to see how to use the trends, once we have them, to forecast.

Using the same notation, let's say we have some data series y that represents the historic stock prices. We have used our "argmin" to produce the best trend model that describes how y behaves up to some given time T where we stand now.

What I really want to know is where y, my stock price, will be *h* time steps forward in the future based on the model I currently have. This is still regression, so we know when we look forward we will have some random error term.

So I am going to modify this equation:

$$T_t = \beta_0 + \beta_1 \text{TIME}_t$$

to look ahead *h* steps in time.

$$y_{T+h} = \beta_0 + \beta_1 \text{TIME}_{T+h} + \varepsilon_{T+h}$$

So now this says our "stock price" that we are calling *y* at some time in the future will follow our existing model plus some time step forward, *h*, plus the assumed error term around the regression.

Although messy, this should make sense. We want to predict our stock price from now plus some time step forward based on our super model we created and know that with all regressions there will be some standard error of the trend repressors, sigma.

Finally, the answer: If we want to form an interval forecast, we assume some variability across the interval, let's say 95% for simplicity, so we have a *z* score of 1.96. So far, so good.

This all reduces to:

$$\hat{y}_{T+h}, T \pm 1.96\hat{\sigma}$$

So *y* hat is our estimate of where we are now (*T*) plus some time step *h* plus or minus sigma hat, which is standard error of the trend regression, an estimator for the true value of sigma.

Notice none of these learning objectives are calculating, but the disappointing answer to using trends as a forecast is basically where you are now plus or minus the *z*-score of how certain you want to be multiplied by the variability of the regression.

This is basically another way to express random walk, but if you don't go through all the pain of this new notation it may not make sense for you later on.

QUANTITATIVE ANALYSIS (QA)

Learning objective: Compare and evaluate model selection criteria, including mean squared error (MSE), s^2, the Akaike information criterion (AIC), and the Schwarz information criterion (SIC).

To penalize the squared error method (*s*-squared), we need to add a term to describe the degrees of freedom to the original equation, which becomes:

$$s^2 = \frac{\sum_{t=1}^{T} e_t^2}{T-k}$$

Because of the previously discussed relationship between mean squared error and *R*-squared, we modify *R*-squared with the same term *k* for degrees of freedom.

$$MSE = \frac{\sum_{t=1}^{T} e_t^2}{T}$$

$$e_t = y_t - \hat{y}_t$$

$$\hat{y}_t = \hat{\beta}_0 + \hat{\beta}_1 \, TIME_t$$

So our adjusted *R*-squared gets penalized for degrees of freedom, too:

$$\bar{R}^2 = 1 - \frac{\sum_{t=1}^{T} e_t^2 / (T-k)}{\sum_{t=1}^{T}(y_t - \bar{y})^2 / (T-1)} = 1 - \frac{s^2}{\sum_{t=1}^{T}(y_t - \bar{y})^2 / (T-1)}$$

It's easy to get lost in the math, so let's step back. We are trying to develop a model to predict future data from the data we have in hand. We can create a model that predicts the current data well. Let's say we have a few models that predict the data well, all by looking at the MSE.

We want to penalize the models we are choosing from in a consistent way with the knowledge that additional degrees of freedom (additional regressors in our model) have a higher predictive power due to possible spurious correlation and not necessarily greater predictive power. We want to find the middle ground that has a high predictive power but not too many factors so that we question the value of the model. The "penalty" in the mean squared error construct is just to reduce the sample size *T* by the degrees of freedom *k*.

Now we have two more penalty values that modify the original MSE formula by multiplying by a factor.

Those formulas are:

$$AIC = e^{\left(\frac{2k}{T}\right)} \frac{\sum_{t=1}^{T} e_t^2}{T}$$

$$SIC = T^{\left(\frac{k}{T}\right)} \frac{\sum_{t=1}^{T} e_t^2}{T}$$

You don't need to memorize these, just know what they are and perhaps recognize that for large degrees of freedom, the factor on SIC will increase faster than AIC.

Learning objective: Explain the necessary conditions for a model selection criterion to demonstrate consistency.

There is an idea called consistency that requires two properties.

1. Think of a whole bunch of different models varying predictive capacity of the actual value we are modeling. As we add more and more models (not regressors—new models) the probability of selecting the right one approaches 1, meaning it is obvious which model produced the data.
2. If we have a bunch of models but don't include the actual model in the analysis, as we add more and more models the probability of finding the best approximation to the actual model approaches 1.

Keep in mind, this applies only to in-sample data and really depends on the degrees of freedom in the model—we want to penalize for DoF to reduce the chance of picking a model due to spurious correlation is all the model selection criteria is about.

Diebold, Chapter 6

Francis X. Diebold, *Elements of Forecasting*, 4th Edition (Mason, Ohio: Cengage Learning, 2006). Chapter 6. Modeling and Forecasting Seasonality

After completing this reading, you should be able to:

- Describe the sources of seasonality and how to deal with it in time series analysis.
- Explain how to use regression analysis to model seasonality.
- Explain how to construct an *h*-step-ahead point forecast.

Learning objective: Describe the sources of seasonality and how to deal with it in time series analysis.

The technical definition of seasonality is a repeating pattern every year. There are two types: deterministic, which is an exact repletion; or stochastic, which is an approximate representation of the pattern either around the same time or magnitude.

Seasonality can come from a lot of places but mostly comes because humans change their behavior around seasons. Buy more gas in the summer, devote more energy toward agriculture in the summer, electricity demand, and so forth. Financial assets have seasonality too. Asset rebalancing, durable goods orders, inventory management all have financial seasonality.

The questions are: How to manage that seasonality and know when data begins to diverge from known seasonality? How significant those divergences may be? What may the divergences imply from the markets?

One of the easiest ways to deal with seasonality in a time series of data is to acknowledge the seasonality and remove it, leaving us with what is called a seasonally adjusted time series. The one problem here is that if the seasonality is a large driver of the divergence of the series, meaning the bulk of the information comes from how the series season changes, we remove some of the informational advantage that time series analysis gives us.

Learning objective: Explain how to use regression analysis to model seasonality.

To fix this, we use something called regressing on seasonal dummies. A "dummy" variable simply means that if an observation is in a particular category, that variable is given a value of 1 or 0 and they are mutually exclusive.

If we are observing men and women in a study in which being male or female matters to the outcome, then we could create two dummy variables and given our observation—being male or female—a value of 0 or 1.

When we have the results of the regression, the coefficient on the dummy variable shows how much difference it makes to be in category 1, rather than category 0.

Now the example of men and women and the assignment of a one or zero is easy because there are only two observations. What if we had four segments of income and wanted to see how being in any income segment impacted the highest level of education attained? We would have four dummy variables—one for each level of income. If we arranged income from lowest to highest it would look like this:

$$D_1 = (1,0,0,0)$$
$$D_2 = (0,1,0,0)$$
$$D_3 = (0,0,1,0)$$
$$D_4 = (0,0,0,1)$$

Where the dummy variable is (in this case denoted by the number 1) in the first, second, third, or fourth place has different meaning. A dummy in the first spot equals the lowest income and a dummy in the last spot equals highest income.

Now how do we set up our regression equation? Even though we have four dummy variables, our regression equation can only use three of our dummy variables. Now why is this?

Our intent in regression analysis is to see the impact being in one category makes versus not being in that category. So by leaving one category out, the coefficient on the remaining variables is the impact of being in that category versus the omitted variable.

In our example our regression equation might look like this:

$$\text{Highest Education} = a + b*D_1 + c*D_3 + d*D_4 + \varepsilon$$

The omitted variable here is the second one; a is the intercept of the regression; and the coefficients b, c, and d, would be the difference that being in the first, third, or fourth wealth group would make relative to being in the omitted group, the second one.

Notice this isn't a calculate learning objective, so don't waste time doing regression problems when you don't have to.

Learning objective: Explain how to construct an h-step-ahead point forecast.

Regression analysis on historic data tells us nothing about the future. The intent with the h-step forward regression is to see how we can apply historical results and see how we can predict the future.

This is very simple, but the simplicity also makes an h-step look-ahead regression model assuming our model variables are normally distributed. At the 95% level of confidence, we would "disturb" or move the regression variable by +/− 1.96σ.

I think what GARP wants you to know here is that we can very precisely define a regression of historical data and even control for seasonality, but when we begin to use trend analysis for forecasting, we are still reliant upon how our regression coefficients change according to the normal distribution.

Diebold, Chapter 7

Francis X. Diebold, *Elements of Forecasting*, 4th Edition (Mason, Ohio: Cengage Learning, 2006). Chapter 7. Characterizing Cycles

After completing this reading you should be able to:

- Define covariance stationary, autocovariance function, autocorrelation function, partial autocorrelation function, and autoregression.
- Describe the requirements for a series to be covariance stationary.
- Explain the implications of working with models that are not covariance stationary.
- Define white noise, describe independent white noise and normal (Gaussian) white noise.
- Explain the characteristics of the dynamic structure of white noise.
- Explain how a lag operator works.
- Describe Wold's theorem.
- Define a general linear process.
- Relate rational distributed lags to Wold's theorem.
- Calculate the sample mean and sample autocorrelation, and describe the Box-Pierce Q-statistic and the Ljung-Box Q-statistic.
- Describe sample partial autocorrelation.

Learning objective: Define covariance stationary, autocovariance function, autocorrelation function, partial autocorrelation function, and autoregression.

Learning objective: Describe the requirements for a series to be covariance stationary.

Learning objective: Explain the implications of working with models that are not covariance stationary.

COVARIANCE STATIONARY FUNCTION

When an independent variable in the regression equation is a lagged value of the dependent variable (as is the case in autoregressive time series models) statistical inferences based on OLS regression are not always valid. In order to conduct statistical inference based on these models, we must assume that the time series is covariance stationary or weakly stationary. There are three basic requirements for a time series to be covariance stationary:

1. The expected value or mean of the time series must be constant and finite in all periods.
2. The variance of the time series must be constant and finite in all periods.
3. The covariance of the time series with itself for a fixed number of periods in the past or future must be constant and finite in all periods.

It is a good time to note what type of time series is not mean stationary: if the time series has a trend line such as GDP growth or employment, by definition that time series is not mean stationary. Same thing with variance—if the time series has a trending or changing variance, it is not variance stationary.

For notation in this reading we are going to use

$$E(y_t) = \mu$$

to say the expectation of our sample path *y* is the mean of *y*. In other words, rule number 1.

AUTOCOVARIANCE FUNCTION

To determine if our series has a stable covariance structure over different periods of time we have to use an autocovariance function. Series analysis is usually limited to time series in finance but it can apply to any type of data. We refer to a "displacement" as the next step in a series be it three-dimensional data or linear time series data.

We need to include displacement and time in our autocovariance function like:

$$\gamma(t, \tau) = \gamma(\tau)$$

This just says our function has two variables, time and displacement, and the covariance between those two equals the expectation of each of them minus the mean, which from step one we assume to be zero. In order to be covariance stationary, the series cannot be dependent upon time, which reduces our autocorrelation equation to reduce to be dependent just on displacement:

$$\gamma(t, \tau) = \text{cov}(y_t, y_{t-\tau}) = E(y_t - \mu)(y_{t-\tau} - \mu)$$

AUTOCORRELATION FUNCTION

Now, just like covariance in other areas of analysis doesn't tell us much—there are no units, it can vary widely, etc.—we use correlation to normalize covariance. Recall that we calculate correlation by dividing covariance by standard deviation, and just in the same way we create the correlation function, we divide our autocovariance function by standard deviation.

When the autocorrelations are plotted by time step—we can graphically see how the dependence pattern changes or alters by lag step.

Learning objective: Define white noise, describe independent white noise and normal (Gaussian) white noise.

White noise is a special characterization of a type of error terms within a time series. Recall we use "y" to denote an observed time series and we further want to say the error terms have a mean 0 and some known, constant variance.

Formulaically,

$$y_t = \epsilon_t$$
$$\epsilon_t \sim (0, \sigma^2)$$

Furthermore, if the error terms are uncorrelated over time, that process is called white noise. If we can further show that the series *y* is independent and identically distributed, the white noise becomes independent white noise. Lastly, if we can show i.i.d as well as normally distributed, we say the white noise is Gaussian (normally distributed).

Learning objective: Explain the characteristics of the dynamic structure of white noise.

It is important to understand that white noise is uncorrelated over time, has zero autocorrelation, and is basically a random stochastic process. The take-away from this reading is that forecast errors should be white noise—and this is counterintuitive—because if the errors aren't white noise then the errors are serially correlated, which also means the errors are forecastable, which also means the forecast itself is flawed or unreliable.

Learning objective: Explain how a lag operator works.

Since we are manipulating time series data to explain how the past evolves into the future, we have to manipulate the forecast model and a lag operator will turn the current one into the previous observation like this:

$$Ly_t = y_{t-1}$$

A lag of two steps would have *L* raised to the second power and so forth. For now, just know the notation. We will get into the reason, use, and meaning later.

$$L^2 y_t = LLy_t = Ly_{t-1} = y_{t-2}$$

so the first lag of our autocovariance equation would look like this:

$$\gamma(1) = \operatorname{cov}(Y_t, Y_{t-1})$$
$$= E((Y_t - \mu)(Y_{t-1} - \mu))$$

You can visualize a lag by taking any graph and "shifting" the entire chart by one or more time steps—however large the lag may be.

Now, we can also lag a time series by a polynomial where we set the observation at *t* plus some fraction of prior observations like this:

$$(1 + .14L + .06^2)\, y_t = y_t + .14_{t-1} + 0.6_{t-2}$$

Learning objective: Describe Wold's theorem.

Time series analysis is all about picking the right model to fit a series of data. When we have a set of data that is covariance stationary there are a lot of model choices that could fit the data with different degrees of effectiveness. This alone doesn't tell us anything about whether or not this is the right model. Think of this idea as analogous to correlation doesn't equal causation. This breaks down the time series into two pieces—one deterministic and one stochastic (a.k.a. random or white noise) so Wold's theorem is the model of the covariance stationary residual.

Time series models are constructed as linear functions of fundamental forecasting errors, also called innovations or shocks.

These basic building blocks of models are the same: mean 0 with some known variance, serially uncorrelated, a.k.a. white noise. In this sense, all errors are white noise and unforecastable.

Now, in this reading the error terms are often referred to as "innovations," which gets very confusing. The reason this came about is because if we have an actual error, not white noise, in a time series, then that actually introduces new information to the system that can be modeled, can be predicted, and is in some way correlated to the rest of the time series.

Furthermore, a "distributed lag" is a weighted sum of previous values that factor in some way to our estimation of the current value of the time series, which is exactly what the equation from the last learning objective is—a distributed lag, meaning the current value weight is distributed over several previous values of the time series.

Recall the exponentially weighted model where we set lambda at some value to drive the "decay" of the informational value of the historical data. If we want to grab all historical value, it's called infinitely distributable.

The formula looks like this:

$$y_t = B(L)\epsilon_t = \sum_{i=0}^{\infty} b_i \epsilon_{t-1}$$

$$\epsilon_t \sim WN(0, \sigma^2)$$

Learning objective: Define a general linear process.

This reading is quite complicated and it is easy to get bogged down in formulas when all they are asking for is a definition. In this case, a general linear process describes Wold's theorem because the previous formula is a series of linear functions and its "innovations." This is probably a low probability for the exam.

Learning objective: Relate rational distributed lags to Wold's theorem.

There are two types of lags in time series analysis: infinite and finite. In an infinite series, we assume all data in the past has an impact on the dependent variable we are modeling so it is "infinitely distributed." Same for a finite distribution, we just have to define how many lagged periods impact the time series. In these types of lagged models, we assume there is some weight applied to each lag but there can also be polynomials in the lag factor. The problem arises because models with an infinite number of parameters can't be estimated from a finite sample of data. However, an infinite polynomial in the lag operator won't necessarily have infinite free parameters. We can have an infinite series of polynomials that only depend on, say, two parameters. A rational distributed lag is the ratio of the parameters in the infinitely distributed lag so that we can approximate an infinitely lagged series from a finite sample of data, which is how we recover Wold's theorem from rational distributed lags.

Learning objective: Calculate the sample mean and sample autocorrelation, and describe the Box-Pierce Q-statistic and the Ljung-Box Q-statistic.

Recall that when we are dealing with any type of "sample" we are dealing with estimators, not parameters, and we extend the mean and autocorrelation to accommodate that we know there is some degree of error in the estimator. This is called replacing expectations with sample averages. If we have a sample size of T, the sample mean is calculated as:

$$\bar{y} = \frac{1}{T} \sum_{t=2}^{T} y_t$$

This is not interesting in itself but we can use it to calculate the sample autocorrelation function, which we calculate as:

$$\hat{\rho}(\tau) = \frac{\frac{1}{T} \sum_{t=\tau+1}^{T} ((y_t - \bar{y})(y_{t-\tau} - \bar{y}))}{\frac{1}{T} \sum (y_t - \bar{y})^2} = \frac{\sum_{t=\tau+1}^{T} ((y_t - \bar{y})(y_{t-\tau} - \bar{y}))}{\sum_{t=1}^{T} (y_t - \bar{y})^2}$$

Learning objective: Describe sample partial autocorrelation.

This is a low priority for the exam and is only a "describe learning statement." Instead of obtaining partial autocorrelations in a "thought experiment" of infinite regressions on an infinite data set, we now perform the same on a thought experiment on a more manageable, finite data set and that is why it is called a "sample." This is purely theoretical and a near zero chance on exam day.

Diebold, Chapter 8

Francis X. Diebold, *Elements of Forecasting*, 4th Edition (Mason, Ohio: Cengage Learning, 2006). Chapter 8. Modeling Cycles: MA, AR, and ARMA Models

After completing this reading you should be able to:

- Describe the properties of the first-order moving average (MA(1)) process, and distinguish between autoregressive representation and moving average representation.
- Describe the properties of a general finite-order process of order q (MA(q)) process.
- Describe the properties of the first-order autoregressive (AR(1)) process, and define and explain the Yule-Walker equation.
- Describe the properties of a general pth order autoregressive (AR(p)) process.
- Define and describe the properties of the autoregressive moving average (ARMA) process.
- Describe the application of AR and ARMA processes.

Learning objective: Describe the properties of the first-order moving average (MA(1)) process, and distinguish between autoregressive representation and moving average representation.

The number one in (MA(1)) refers to a lag of one step where our process depends on one error term (also called disturbances or innovations in the readings) to fit previous data and predict what may happen in the future. A one lag series implies only the most recent information is considered in what we expect to happen to the series of data next.

It looks like this:

$$y_t = \epsilon_t + \theta \epsilon_{t-1}$$
$$\epsilon_t \sim WN(0, \sigma^2)$$

We have a process that depends on some disturbance term and some constant theta applied to previous terms. Stated differently, our moving average has a "memory" of only one period and more distance time series don't enter into our conditional expectation calculations.

We also assume the mean is zero just like before, which looks like:

$$E(y_t) = E(\epsilon_t) + \theta E(\epsilon_{t-1}) = 0$$

All we are doing is taking our original equation for the moving order process and adding the expectation terms. Notice that theta comes outside of $E(\ )$ because it is a constant.

And we do the same with variance:

$$\text{Var}(y_t) = \text{var}(\epsilon_t) + \theta^2 \text{var}(\epsilon_{t-1})$$
$$\downarrow \quad \downarrow \quad \downarrow$$
$$= \sigma^2 + \theta^2 \sigma^2$$
$$= \sigma^2(1+\sigma^2)$$
$$= \text{var}(y_t)$$

To compute the autocorrelation function, we start with the autocovariance function just like before.

$$\gamma(0) = \text{COV}(y_t, y_t) = \text{var}(y_t)$$

This reading is a little confusing because we have y as above, which is our moving average process, but we also have the autocovariance function gamma whose symbol is the Greek lowercase "g" but looks like a "y" (not to be confused with any other gamma—it's just the symbol used for the autocovariance function) like this:

$$y(0) = \text{cove } y \, y$$

In words this says, "The autocovariance function with zero displacement is equal to the covariance among the same terms which reduces just to the variance."

This is going to be used a lot in this reading because to normalize covariance we have to divide by the variance and in the moving average nomenclature you will "divide by variance" often.

To complete the autocovariance function for the MA(1) process, we have to compute the autocovariance just like we have done before except this time we are looking at the correlation between the process and its one-step lag. It looks like this:

$$\gamma(\tau) = E(y_t y_{t-\tau}) = E((\epsilon_t \, \theta \epsilon_{t-1})(\epsilon_{t-1} + \theta \epsilon_{t-\tau-1}))$$
$$= \begin{cases} \theta \sigma^2 & \tau = 1 \\ 0, & \text{otherwise} \end{cases}$$

All this says is the autoregression function at tau is dependent upon the two observed y terms, which we have defined as an error term plus some fixed coefficient theta. Notice the far right term:

$$\theta \epsilon_{t-\tau-1}))$$

This is now two steps behind, which means it has zero value and drops out which reduces to the variances (error terms) times each other and that is how we get theta sigma squared where tau equals one.

That leaves us with the autocorrelation function for MA(1).

$$\rho(\tau) = \frac{\gamma(\tau)}{\gamma(0)} = \begin{cases} \frac{\theta}{1+\theta^2}, & \tau = 1 \\ 0, & \text{otherwise} \end{cases}$$

Learning objective: Describe the properties of a general pth order autoregressive (AR(p)) process.

Learning objective: Describe the properties of a general finite-order process of order q (MA(q)) process.

So this just means we are adding more lags. And q could equal 2 or 100 and the properties would remain the same: MA(q) is covariance stationary, MA(q) has a longer "memory" so the mean is conditional upon q previous steps. The general form behaves just like the special case of MA(1) and the same is for AR(p).

Learning objective: Describe the properties of the first-order autoregressive (AR(1)) process, and define and explain the Yule-Walker equation.

Keep in mind, with any analysis of the time series, we are trying to uncover what type of process is spitting out the observed data and then choose what might be the best model to determine future values—the out of sample—or future data.

Just like MA(1), AR(1) has a mean of zero and a constant variance so those properties are the same. Where AR(1) will vary from MA(1) is in the correlation structure and the behavior around the "decay" of old information. For the exam just know that the Yule-Walker equation shows that an autoregressive process—the more it is displaced—the less value is placed on previous error terms.

Learning objective: Define and describe the properties of the autoregressive moving average (ARMA) process.

ARMA models attempt to combine MA(q) and AR(q) models because the random disturbances themselves are moving averages. This is an attempt at the best of both worlds and at improving forecasting ability.

What you really need to know is the mean is time varying. This is important for the regime-shifting analysis of volatility like we have discussed before. However, unlike the AR(q) MA(q) that ignores information beyond our q-lag, the ARMA model decays away almost like an exponentially moving average. Also since ARMA(p,q) has more variables, they can be a better fit but any mis-specification can result in large errors.

Learning objective: Describe the application of AR and ARMA processes.

The AR process is where we begin to see the upper limit of math complexity because we are using a stochastic, or random, process to create noise around the previous value. This is another name for a random walk process. An ARMA process is an AR process but where we assume the random error we are "bumping" the previous value, which is itself a moving average. Both of these models are used to model a wide array of economic systems—everything from serial economic data to other "stochastic" processes.

HULL, CHAPTER 10

John C. Hull, *Risk Management and Financial Institutions*, 4th ed.
(Hoboken, NJ: John Wiley & Sons, 2015). Chapter 10. Volatility

After completing this reading you should be able to:

- Define and distinguish between volatility, variance rate, and implied volatility.
- Describe the power law.
- Explain how various weighting schemes can be used in estimating volatility.
- Apply the exponentially weighted moving average (EWMA) model to estimate volatility.
- Describe the generalized autoregressive conditional heteroskedasticity (GARCH(p,q)) model for estimating volatility and its properties.
    - Calculate volatility using the GARCH(1,1) model.
    - Explain mean reversion and how it is captured in the GARCH(1,1) model.
- Explain the weights in the EWMA and GARCH(1,1) models.
- Explain how GARCH models perform in volatility forecasting.
- Describe the volatility term structure and the impact of volatility changes.

Learning objective: Define and distinguish between volatility, variance rate, and implied volatility.

With all the discussion on volatility and variance on the FRM exam, it is often easy to actually forget what 18% annualized volatility actually means. So this is a good spot to revisit.

Volatility is the standard deviation of return per unit of time assuming continuous compounding. If we are talking about asset pricing, the range of time could be six months or it could be one year. In risk management, the time scale is usually much shorter, on the order of days.

If an asset has a price of $50 and a daily volatility of 1%, what does that even mean in terms of possible range of outcomes? It means the one standard deviation change in price of this asset over one day could be $50 * .01 = $1.

This potential volatility tells us nothing about direction of change or even how certain we are that change could occur. If we assume a normal distribution, then our range of outcomes is $50 – 1.96 * 1 = $48.04 and $50 + 1.96 * 1 = $51.96.

Volatility is then just the potential range of outcomes. The variance rate, by contrast, is the square of the volatility. Stated differently, the variance rate *per day* is the variance *of the return* in one day. This is where our infamous square root rule by time comes from and we will see more of that later.

Learning objective: Learning objective: Explain how various weighting schemes can be used in estimating volatility.

We can define volatility as a standard deviation of the continuously compounded returns over some period of time. We can examine volatility both within the context of equity returns, commodity prices, or interest-rate movements.

The key property to understand is what model we are applying to the forward distribution of volatility (which we will discuss later) and also consider the proper use of a normal versus lognormal model.

The basic treatment of volatility is that historical volatility can in some way indicate how volatility will behave in the future. This is the key property within the context of predicting future volatility. The one key problem with this in the real world is that volatility is often a canary in the coal mine where large spikes in volatility presage extreme events.

So how does this work in the real world? To say that you are long or short volatility typically implies that you are long or short options on some underlying asset. If volatility is going higher, we must be clear if we are referring to real volatility or implied volatility. An historical or realized volatility seeks to mathematically define the variation of returns of an asset and is exclusively backward looking.

Volatility models then use this backward-looking measure to somehow extrapolate what behavior we may expect in the future. This is the idea of the weighting schemes that we will talk about further on. More important, however, is the behavior of implied volatility. This type of volatility describes what market participants currently are willing to pay for what is effectively insurance, whatever the underlying asset may be.

Therefore, if implied volatility is moving higher, it means that market participants are willing to pay increasingly higher "insurance premiums" for options that protect against extreme movements or conversely pay off large sums of money and extreme moves.

It is this measure of implied volatility that is in my view more important, and certainly is most sensitive to potential future extreme events. One way of examining the relative impact of historical volatility on our estimation of current implied volatility is to use a weighting scheme that attaches more value to recent data points than data points that are further away. This is a very intuitive way of saying that we are giving more weight to the most recent information that the market has about the volatility of the underlying asset. By extension, we can say that given a large number of observations, historical observed volatility could give insight to a "long run" or "steady state" estimate for volatility.

Learning objective: Apply the exponentially weighted moving average (EWMA) model to estimate volatility.

ARCH(M) MODEL

The ARCH(M) model is one where a market participant is predicting the long run or steady state of volatility by first starting with some long-term average of volatility and then including some weighted average to the most recent data points. For example, if the last five trading sessions had indicated eight sessions of upward pressure on volatility above the long-run trend, the arch model would capture this and include both the long-run constant as well as some weight given to the most recent information from the market.

The exponentially weighted moving average is a special case of the ARCH(M) model where the weight given to historical data decreases or decays away at an exponentially increasing rate. In an exponentially weighted moving average of model, the parameter is a constant between zero and one, can be interpreted as a percentage, and describes how quickly older data decays away. The implication is that a higher parameter will discount increasingly older data points at an increasingly higher rate.

ESTIMATING VOLATILITY USING THE EWMA MODEL

Keep in mind this is not a calculate question. So I think what they are looking for is what would happen to an exponentially weighted moving average estimate of volatility should one change the parameters, that is, the exponential weighting. So here's what you need to know for the exam: An exponentially moving weighted average estimate of volatility with a lower lambda which means greater weight will be given to older periods. The data will be slower to recognize "breakouts" for estimates of volatility. Alternatively, exponentially moving weighted average models with high lambdas or greater weight given to more recent data points and almost no weight given to historical data points will capture the large, recent moves in volatility quicker. There is an obvious trade-off in that a model that gives weight only to recent data points is more noisy than one that includes a steady-state constant volatility with more data points contributing to current estimates of volatility.

Learning objective: Describe the generalized auto regressive conditional heteroskedasticity (GARCH(p,q)) model for estimating volatility and its properties:

- **Calculate volatility using the GARCH(1,1) model**

- **Explain mean reversion and how it is captured in the GARCH(1,1) model**

If a model assumes that the error term behaves according to an autoregressive moving average model, then the event model is assumed to be a generalized autoregressive conditional heteroskedasticity model. If we were to set p and q equal to 1, then the GARCH(1,1) model would have a leptokurtic distribution.

CALCULATING VOLATILITY USING THE GARCH(1,1) MODEL

It is most likely you will be given the values of the GARCH equation and expected to know how to use them. First, you need to know the equation:

$$\sigma_n^2 = \gamma V_L + \alpha U_{n-1}^2 + \beta \sigma_{n-1}^2$$

So volatility is equal to the long-run average volatility, where U is the day-over-day change in the asset price, and beta is the weight given to the volatility in the previous time step. Notice each of the three variables has a weight and they need to add up to one to be consistent.

GARCH(1,1) can also be written:

$$\sigma_n^2 = \omega + \alpha U_{n-1}^2 + \beta \sigma_{n-1}^2$$

where ω is the weight given to the long-run average of volatility.

EXPLAINING MEAN REVERSION AND HOW IT IS CAPTURED IN THE GARCH(1,1) MODEL

Mean Reversion

A time series is said to exhibit mean reversion if it tends to fall when its current level is above the mean and tends to rise when its current level is below the mean. The mean-reverting level, x_1, for a time series is given as:

$$x_t = \frac{b_0}{1 - b_1}$$

- If a time series is currently at its mean-reverting level, the model predicts that its value will remain unchanged in the next period.
- If a time series is currently above its mean-reverting level, the model predicts that its value will decrease in the next period.
- If a time series is currently below its mean-reverting level, the model predicts that its value will increase in the next period.

Important: All covariance stationary time series have a finite mean-reverting level. An AR(1) time series will have a finite mean-reverting level if the absolute value of the lag coefficient, b_1, is less than 1.

Learning objective: Explain the weights in the EWMA and GARCH (1,1) models.

In order to understand the weights within the models, we start with the most recent form of GARCH(1,1) in the previous example. Conceptually, we want to arrive at a place where it is clear that beta is a "decay" factor where we quantify the relative importance of each previous step. The decay is exponential so if we have a beta of .80 in one step then in $n-1$ it is 80 squared and so on.

$$\sigma_n^2 = \omega + \alpha U_{n-1}^2 + \beta \sigma_{n-1}^2$$

Substituting for σ_{n-2}^2 gives

$$\sigma_n^2 = \omega + \alpha u_{n-1}^2 + \beta(\omega + \alpha u_{n-2}^2 + \beta \sigma_{n-2}^2)$$

or

$$\sigma_n^2 = \omega + \beta\omega + \alpha u_{n-1}^2 + \alpha\beta u_{n-2}^2 + \beta^2 \sigma_{n-2}^2$$

Substituting for σ_{n-2}^2 gives

$$\sigma_n^2 = \omega + \beta\omega + \beta^2\omega + \alpha u_{n-1}^2 + \alpha\beta u_{n-2}^2 + \alpha\beta^2 u_{n-3}^2 + \beta^3 u_{n-3}^2$$

If we continue this pattern and pay attention to beta, which is the most recent change in our market variable, it becomes clear that beta is the decayed weight applied and explicitly represents the information value that we attribute to old data in predicting future moves.

Learning objective: Explain how GARCH models perform in volatility forecasting.

Keep in mind that the key distinction within the GARCH model is that volatility is a function of time. More specifically, the volatility changes with time.

The key value of the model itself is its ability to remove autocorrelation from a series of data. Think of autocorrelation as the seasonality of a relationship.

By removing that autocorrelation we can look at the "true" patterns within the time series data. The GARCH model does a good job of this, and specifically the value of the GARCH model can be tested by what is called the Ljung-Box statistic.

This is the key idea for the exam: GARCH does a good job of removing autocorrelation from the time series data, so it does a good job in explaining the data. This is a key point. So far we have only looked at the GARCH model to explain the historical data that we have. We now begin to look at methodology to predict volatility and how effective these models are in translating historical volatility input into predictions of future volatility.

Learning objective: Describe the volatility term structure and the impact of volatility changes.

Just like yield curves have a term structure, volatility does too. The reason it is called a "surface" is because the term structure is three dimensional due to the addition of an extra axis—volatility is a function of time to expiration of the option, strike price, and the term of the instrument after the option. For example, a 1Y10Y is a 1-year option on 10-year swap rates and the strike would be modeled on the vertical axis.

The volatility surface changes when the market price for options change. We see this in the change in implied volatility and that is what the surface reflects. As volatility changes, it impacts the price of optionality in the same way: higher volatility equals higher cost to insure against adverse moves.

Learning objective: Describe how correlations and covariances are calculated, and explain the consistency condition for covariances.

This learning objective is a repeat from the Miller, Chapter 3 reading with the exception of the consistency condition, which is very straightforward: the consistency condition simply says if we calculate variances using a GARCH(1,1) with a beta of .80, then we should also use the same assumption when calculating covariances. The reading goes into a bit more detail on a positive-semidefinite property that gets into matrix algebra that is beyond the scope of the FRM exam.

HULL, CHAPTER 11

John Hull, *Risk Management and Financial Institutions,* 4th Edition (New York: John Wiley & Sons, 2015). Chapter 11. Correlations and Copulas

After completing this reading you should be able to:

- Define correlation and covariance, differentiate between correlation and dependence.
- Calculate covariance using the EWMA and GARCH (1,1) models.
- Apply the consistency condition to covariance.
- Describe the procedure for generating samples from a bivariate normal distribution.
- Describe properties of correlations between normally distributed variables when using a one-factor model.
- Define copula, describe the key properties of copula and copula correlation.
- Explain one-tail dependence.
- Describe Gaussian copula, student t-copula, multivariate copula, and one-factor copula.

Learning objective: Define correlation and covariance, differentiate between correlation and dependence.

The **covariance of returns** is an absolute measure of two random variables moving together relative to their individual mean values over time.

A positive covariance means that returns for two investments tend to move in the same direction, while a negative covariance implies that the returns tend to move in opposite directions.

The definition of **correlation**, in terms of covariance, is:

$$\rho_{x,y} = \frac{\text{Cov}(x, y)}{\sigma_x \sigma_y}$$

This isn't a "calculate" learning objective, but you will need to memorize this for exam day.

The distinction between correlation and dependence is related to our knowledge about the cause of an event. If we are sure x will only happen or change given y, then that is said to be dependent. Correlation on the other hand can tell us that two things are changing together but tells us nothing about the cause. This is the origin of the phrase "correlation is not causation."

Learning objective: Calculate covariance using the EWMA and GARCH (1,1) models.

I think on the exam they will give you the "normal" covariance and you will have to modify it according to the EWMA and GARCH in the right way.

© 2017 Wiley

There are two formulas you need to know for the calculation:

$$COV_n = \lambda COV_{n-1} + (1-\lambda) X_{n-1} Y_{n-1}$$

$$COV_n = \omega + \alpha x_{n-1} + Y_{n-1} + \beta cov_{n-1}$$

For EWMA, they will give you the lambda term and it represents the decay in value the model applies to that volatility data. The theory is that the information value of recent volatility data is more important than old data.

If the correlation between two variables is 60% and the volatility of each variable is 2% and 3% respectively, this gives us .00036 covariance just using the standard correlation/covariance relationship. The idea with EWMA is we want to update this with new information including lambda.

Let's say the next day move on both assets was 2% and we want to update our volatility estimate using EWMA it would look like this:

$$\sigma_{x,n}^2 = 0.85 * 0.02^2 + 0.15 * 0.02^2 = 0.00006$$
$$\sigma_{y,n}^2 = 0.85 * 0.032^2 + 0.15 * 0.02^2 = 0.000825$$
$$cov_n = .85 * .00036 + 0.05 * 0.02 * 0.03 = .000336$$

Therefore, the new covariance is .000336.

Learning objective: Apply the consistency condition to covariance.

The consistency condition for covariance refers to the idea that variances and covariance should be calculated consistently. By consistently, I mean that if variances are calculated using an exponentially weighted moving average model with lamda equal to .75, then the same thing should be done for the covariance calculation.

Learning objective: Describe the procedure of generating samples from a bivariate normal distribution.

Just like many computers have random number generators, many problems in finance require simulated normal distributions—most notably, a Monte Carlo simulation.

This is a "describe" learning objective and the math can be quite technical, so don't get bogged down in the technicals. First, a bivariate normal distribution is one where two random variables, when added together, are still normal. You have heard me say normal distributions add linearly and this is what I am referring to. This comes up a lot as we simulate future potential asset paths and we want to ensure that the addition of other distributions is still normally distributed.

However, those added distributions do have some degree of correlation. We use that correlation of the bivariate normal distribution to create random samples like this:

1. First take two samples from a bivariate normal and call them Z_1 and Z_2.
2. Our samples will be ϵ_1 and ϵ_2.
3. ϵ_1 we are going to leave alone and leave equal to the first sample Z_1.
4. We create a random sample ϵ_2 by bringing in the correlation of the bivariate normal like this:

$$\epsilon_1 = Z_1$$
$$\epsilon_2 = \rho Z_1 + Z_2 \sqrt{1-\rho^2}$$

I can't imagine that GARP would ask you to calculate anything here, just understand that distributions can be sampled to create other distributions, and you mostly see this in simulations where we have to assume a lot of different price changes over time but also assume some stable distribution.

Learning objective: Describe properties of correlations between normally distributed variables when using a one-factor model.

Imagine we have a series of standard normal distributions. Since this is a one-factor model, each distribution will be dependent upon one common factor, F, and some other elements to the model, such as CAPM, where we have systematic and unsystematic risk driving returns.

Learning objective: Define copula, and describe the key properties of copula and copula correlation.

If we know that two random variables (the price of an asset, for example) are related, the bivariate example from before, we can calculate the correlation structure inherent within those two, or any number, of related distributions.

Consider we notice two different financial products are correlated, but we know nothing about the distribution itself. As long as the random variables we are considering are normally distributed (remember financial products are not, so copulas don't always give correct results), we can use copulas to define the correlation structure without knowing about the distribution itself. This is great when you want to consider any particular joint outcome and still preserve the correlation between the two variables.

Learning objective: Explain one-tail dependence.

Recall how I have said over and over that in times of stress, correlations go to 1. I don't mean this literally, exactly one, but strongly moving in that direction. This is why copula correlation is so important. When correlations move toward 1 in market stress, this moves more "mass" or probability into the tails of the distribution—the rules governing how the asset is expected to price have changed.

Take two assets from two different normal distributions. We will define the tail value as at what z-score the remaining 1% of the distribution in the tails. This is the definition of the 99% level of significance but if we don't know what the probability density function is, we have to estimate it. Fortunately, for the t-distribution and the standard normal, we know what these values are. For the normal distribution we know this is 2.33. The student t-distribution we know has fatter tails and has a z-score of 3.75 at the 99% level of significance.

Learning objective: Describe Gaussian copula, student t-copula, multivariate copula, and one-factor copula.

The Gaussian copula is considered to be the formula that broke Wall Street during the crisis, so if you do have extra time, dig a little deeper into this topic after the exam.

For the exam, here is what you need to know: The law of large numbers tells us we can take samples from any distribution, regardless of the original distribution, and as we take more samples, our sample set will be normally distributed. This is one of the more mind-bending aspects of probability theory. We can know that we don't know a particular distribution but we can know that with a large enough sample size, our sample set will be normally distributed.

Knowing this, we can map the original, unknown, distribution to the known normal distribution. The way this is done is by percentile area under the curve. So the 1% of the unknown distribution is mapped to the 1% of the normal distribution, which we know by standard z-scores. The two new distributions are now normal and we further assumed a joint correlation structure between them.

The Gaussian copula is then the assumption that we can transform unknown, non-normal random variables into a normal distribution from which we can derive a correlation structure. First of all, we are many assumptions deep at this point: Recall how I have said numerous times that in times of stress, correlations go to 1? This is where this becomes problematic—shifting correlations that can't be predicted even with the Gaussian copula.

The student-t copula is one where we map the unknown original distributions to the student-t distribution instead of the normal. This mapping puts more area in the tails and is a little more forgiving than the normal.

Brooks, Chapter 13

Chris Brooks, *Introductory Econometrics for Finance*, 3rd Edition (Cambridge, UK: Cambridge University Press, 2014). Chapter 13. Simulation Methods

After completing this reading you should be able to:

- Describe the basic steps to conduct a Monte Carlo simulation.
- Describe ways to reduce Monte Carlo sampling error.
- Explain how to use antithetic variate technique to reduce Monte Carlo sampling error.
- Explain how to use control variates to reduce Monte Carlo sampling error and when it is effective.
- Describe the benefits of reusing sets of random number draws across Monte Carlo experiments and how to reuse them.
- Describe the bootstrapping method and its advantage over Monte Carlo simulation.
- Describe the pseudo-random number generation method and how a good simulation design alleviates the effects that the choice of the seed has on the properties of the generated series.
- Describe situations where the bootstrapping method is ineffective.
- Describe disadvantages of the simulation approach to financial problem solving.

Learning objective: Describe the basic steps to conduct a Monte Carlo simulation.

There are four steps you need to know for the exam:

1. Have some data generating process (DGP) with errors drawn from some given distribution. This is the idea of a random, stochastic process. With Monte Carlo simulation, we are going to create many potential paths of a future state of the world. The choice of the model that drives the DGP will also be critical to an accurate simulation.
2. We have to define the parameter of interest that we are modeling. Usually this is the return of the asset, but it could be anything.
3. Save the outcome of that scenario (or the entire path if you are modeling mortgage-backed securities).
4. Repeat as many times as possible. Since we have a known DGP and are drawing from some known error distribution, the simulation will also have those similar outcomes.

Learning objective: Describe ways to reduce Monte Carlo sampling error.

This is known as a variance reduction technique. As we have more samples, our sample converges on the population and we have less variance in the estimates of our parameters for the simulation. This isn't the variance or risk of the asset; this is the variance of our sample. That is what we want to reduce. The two ways to do that are the next learning objectives.

Learning objective: Explain how to use antithetic variate technique to reduce Monte Carlo sampling error.

In a Monte Carlo simulation, we are making random pulls from a known distribution of errors. We sample a new error and apply that to the last position, and we have the new step in the simulation. After doing this over and over, we have run only one simulation. We have to estimate each individual time step as well as doing this entire series run over and over.

The reason so many samples have to be made is we need to give the simulation enough time to randomly draw from every possible outcome of the state of the world we are trying to model. Simply running more simulations will reduce our variance of samples, but that takes many draws.

The antithetic variate method will reduce the variance of estimates while keeping the number of simulation runs manageable. In order to do this, for every sample we take we run another simulation starting with the negative value of that sample draw. The reason for this, and how this reduces the variance of error terms, is beyond the scope of the exam, so just know what the technique is and how to use it.

Learning objective: Explain how to use control variates to reduce Monte Carlo sampling error and when it is effective.

In this case, we have some other variable we use in the simulation but we know all the parameters of this new control variate. Instead of turning the sample into its mirror image, we shift the control variate by some simple manipulation. Think of this as shifting the sample by some defined amount. The method of how to estimate how much to manipulate the control variable is beyond the scope of the FRM exam, but know that the control variable should be related to the simulation variable to be effective. We aren't just randomly shifting a sample, but that is the limit of what you need to know for the exam.

Learning objective: Describe the benefits of reusing sets of random number draws across Monte Carlo experiments and how to reuse them.

If we are performing tens of thousands of samples on a known distribution, over time it seems we would have a complete set of the states of the world we are trying to simulate. It seems like a great candidate to save and potentially reuse that computing power without having to run the simulation all over again. The key is that the distribution, error, sampling number, and so on all need to be identical, and if that is the case we are safe to reuse previous path data. Additionally, we can take a segment of a simulation as a shorter simulation. For example, if we modeled mortgage-backed securities over one year but wanted to price the same structured product over a six-month horizon, in theory we could take the first segment of our original population, ignoring all the changes in correlation for this particular product. What you need to know is that, if you are running identical experiments on the same distribution of data, the simulation can be reused and the benefit is saving on computing power.

Learning objective: Describe the bootstrapping method and its advantage over Monte Carlo simulation.

Don't confuse this with bootstrapping a yield curve. With simulations, we use a random number generator to create our starting point, and then bump that value by some errors with known distribution. In this case, we start with some known historical data and some parameter we want to estimate.

We take a sample from the historical data (we don't know the distribution), and from a series of sampling with replacement we infer some distribution around the parameter we are trying to estimate using historical data. This violates all kinds of assumptions we need in finance: most important, the memoryless property within the exponential distribution and the idea of a random walk that portfolio theory is built upon.

Despite the limitations, bootstrapping is much quicker than Monte Carlo simulation and is even better suited for some types of simulation such as in econometrics.

Learning objective: Describe the pseudo-random number generation method and how a good simulation design alleviates the effects that the choice of the seed has on the properties of the generated series.

When starting a simulation, a seed value (state of the world) is chosen to begin the simulation from. For the early stages of the simulation, that choice of the opening state of the world will say more about where the value is, say, five steps from now than where it is 1,000 steps from now. The design of a simulation should run for longer than the simulation actually requires to omit this seed choice bias.

Learning objective: Describe situations where the bootstrapping method is ineffective.

There are only two times when bootstrapping is ineffective: when there are outliers in the data or when there is autocorrelation in the data (the data set is not independent). If outliers appear in the data, bootstrapping doesn't give us any insight into how frequently that outlier appears in the data set since we don't know the distribution we are sampling from. If there is correlation in the data, our estimates of the variation of the distribution will be smaller in simulation and much larger in reality.

Learning objective: Describe disadvantages of the simulation approach to financial problem solving.

- Simulation might be time and computing expensive. Computing costs have come down dramatically in the cloud, so the issue here is time.

- The precision of the simulation rests on the assumptions made in the data generating process. It is highly limited by what could be very subjective assumptions.
- Less important in the real world is the fact that the results are often hard to replicate. This means that, for any given simulation, the valuation of a particular pool of products may vary widely.
- To the previous point, all simulations are event specific. They apply to that state of the world only unless very precise path-dependent records are kept in the instance when we may want to reuse data.